CLASSIC HAULIERS 2

CLASSIC HAULIERS

2

Bob Tuck

The Fitzjames Press

THE FITZJAMES PRESS
an imprint of
Motor Racing Publications Ltd
Unit 6, The Pilton Estate, 46 Pitlake,
Croydon, CR0 3RA, England

First published 1991

British Library Cataloguing in Publication Data
Tuck, Bob
  Classic hauliers 2
  I. Title
  388.3240941

  ISBN 0-948358-03-3

Typeset by Ryburn Typesetting Ltd; origination by
Ryburn Reprographics, Halifax, West Yorkshire

Printed in Great Britain by
The Amadeus Press Limited, Huddersfield,
West Yorkshire

Front cover:

The roots of Marley Transport go back nearly 70 years, and an early
motto of Owen Aisher's for his fledgling tile business, 'Not for an age but
for all time' seems apt when you consider the size and scope of the
modern Marley organisation which has grown from those early
beginnings. The high profile and prestigious image of their current
transport fleet, which will stand comparison with any, has largely evolved
under the command of Managing Director Geoff Lampard, ably backed
by the efforts of a willing staff. The Marley signwriting has undergone
some minor modifications recently, but the tranditional tiler motif remains
and still seems fresh and relevant. The Volvo FL10 in this fine George
Richardson photograph is the regular vehicle of driver Kevin Roberts and
is based at Ebchester, on the boundary of Durham and Northumberland,
a long-established regional base for the company. The Crane Fruehauf
semi-trailer carries a full load of shrink-wrapped roof tiles which are a
standard product of the Ebchester plant.

Back cover:

Munros of Aberdeen have been in the long-distance haulage sector for
almost 40 years and, with branch offices in Glasgow, Manchester and
London, their fleet has been a well known sight in all parts of the UK
mainland. New to some observers is the predominantly white livery
although the long-used Munro yellow is still to be seen on some of the
older vehicles. The change of colour, along with a change in the emphasis
of the company's activities, was brought about by Chief Executive Gordon
Andrews, who was also responsible for bringing British-built vehicles back
into the Munro line-up. H567 USS was new into service in April 1991
and was the first Leyland DAF 80-series to be ordered, fittingly taking
the Munro Fleet total up to the 80 mark. Seen here at Muggie Moss, near
Aberdeen, the unit has Duncan Munro, grandson of the company
founder, behind the wheel. Coupled to one of the latest Boalloy Fineline
curtainsiders on a Montracon chassis, it will be used on a scheduled
overnight trunking service between Aberdeen and Manchester and is
expected to cover some 125,000 miles per year. Supplied by Leyland DAF
dealer Norscott, the truck has the 11.6-litre DAF engine producing
329bhp and driving through an Eaton Twin Splitter 12-speed gearbox.

Contents

Introduction

CLASSIC HAULIERS 2, not surprisingly, follows the formula adopted for the first volume, which many of you were kind enough to say you liked. In making my personal selection of fifteen more road haulage companies to write about, I have again looked for firms with an interesting history and sought to reflect both the diversity of transport tasks that they undertake and the wide scatter of their locations throughout the UK.

The transport industry never stagnates, it is always on the change – that's one reason why it's an attractive subject for a book like this. But it does mean that information relevant at the time of writing can be quickly outdated by changing circumstances. This is particularly true of fleet lists, so where these have been included for currently active companies they should be taken, as before, for general guidance and not as the last word on the subject.

Having been an observer of road haulage for close on 40 years now, I derive considerable pleasure from this opportunity to highlight some of the many fascinating aspects of a varied and vigorous industry that our society would find it impossible to manage without.

Acknowledgements

Producing a book of this nature would not have been possible were it not for the time and consideration afforded to me by all the companies involved. Beyond that general and sizeable debt of gratitude, the following people must be particularly thanked as it is they who have trawled back through the depths of memory to make this volume of special interest: Jimmy and James Adams, Gordon Andrews, Joe Bell, Rex Biggs, Philip Braithwaite, Chris Chaplow, Tom Cobley, David Eastough, Frank Edwards, Norman Gross, Cliff Hedley, Mel Heighway, Geoff Lampard, Ron Lewis, Chris and John Miller, Richard and Anne Preston, Martin Plummer, Richard Read, Pip Sayers, Ron, David and Terry Sinclair, Jock Smith, Norman Smith, George Thomas, David Thompson, Chris Watson, Jim Wilkinson, Alan Woods and Ted Wraight. Of equal assistance in guiding me through many details and problems was the help provided by Glenys Pools, Kay Read and Nora Scott.

The companies themselves were tremendously helpful in supplying many of the photographs used in this book, and invaluable assistance in filling the gaps came from John Easton, Dennis Harris, John Henderson, Malcolm Ladd, Sandy Law, Geoff Milne and John Simons. Special thanks to Paul McNally for his vision in the Marley Tiles cover photograph.

Whilst never forgetting my wife Sylvia who has yet again coaxed me through another contribution to the bookshelves, I would lastly like to mention Roger Kenney. Roger is currently not enjoying the best of health, but his foresight with eye and camera are well known in the ranks of transport enthusiasts. His unselfish help in furnishing material for this book has only reinforced his contribution to the history of the industry and added to the pleasure his work has given to many.

Bob Tuck

Munros began trading in 1933, their localized operations being based in the Mounthooley area of Aberdeen. This Gordon Andrews photograph from the war years is the only known pictorial record of the pre-nationalization fleet. It also illustrates one of the strange modifications some goods vehicles had to undergo when conventional fuel was in short supply. A solid fuel such as wood chips was burnt with a limited air supply to make producer gas on which the suitably modified petrol engine could be persuaded to run.

1: Munros Transport (Aberdeen) Ltd and Maclennans Transport Ltd

Those with any form of interest in fell-walking or mountaineering may well be aware that the term 'Munros' is used to describe the 342 tops of mountains in Scotland which are in excess of 3,000 feet high. But mention the same word in road haulage circles and it is immediately linked with the town of Aberdeen, for the vehicles of Munros Transport have long been a regular sight in all parts of the UK mainland. Although they have depots serving Glasgow, Manchester and London, home and heartland of Munros is very much in the north-east of Scotland. Their St Machar Road complex in Aberdeen stretches to 7 acres and the companies which now fall under the Munro umbrella utilize a fleet which is 80 strong. The Munro name has been affixed to long-distance haulers, mostly maximum-weight outfits, for close on 40 years.

Now into their third generation and currently under the day-to-day control of Managing Director Gordon Andrews, the Munro company has recently been changed in emphasis to reflect a new outlook. Warehousing has been increased in importance and augmenting the backbone of long-distance and trunk vehicles now are vehicles operating a localized distribution network. This perhaps seems fitting when you learn that it was in this line of road transport that Munros first began trading. It was in 1933 that William Duncan Munro started business in the Mounthooley area of Aberdeen. Under the banner of Munros Motor Transport Company he evolved a small fleet of four-wheeled platforms and tippers. Operating on a mixture of 'A' and 'B' carriers' licences, Munros carried all manner of traffic in the north-east area of Scotland.

It wasn't until the end of World War 2 that the company really began to find their feet. First acquiring the three vehicles and goodwill of Speyside Transport Ltd, they went on to buy out the seven-vehicle fleet of Spences Road Transport of Turiff. As befitted a quickly expanding concern, the Munro name was incorporated and changed to

that currently in use, Munros Transport (Aberdeen) Ltd. Running a general haulage fleet that topped the 20 mark, Munros were a natural to be compulsorily taken over when the nationalization wave swept through Aberdeen in 1949. But Duncan Munro had seen it coming and, deciding to broaden his interests, he moved his depot a mile north to the current site on St Machar Road in 1948. The land he bought on a green-field site was far bigger than that required for the then-current fleet – especially one that was soon to disappear into the Government-owned British Road Services – but Munro had plans to use the space and set up a business of motor engineers. This decision was to influence the career of Duncan Munro's son, also called William Duncan Munro, the current Company Chairman, who for a time went to work at Forbes Garage. James M. Forbes (Motors) Ltd still survives today and is currently the main Volvo truck agent for Grampian.

Nationalization or not, Munros were still very much transport people. Late in 1949, Blackhillock Quarry at Keith was bought, a crushing plant installed and Duncan (WDM 2) was put in to run this venture. The company of W.D. Munro Ltd was created and it forged a partnership with North Eastern Farmers to quarry limestone for agricultural use. Although Munros were to be responsible for quarrying, production, distribution and spreading of the lime, North Eastern Farmers were to be responsible for the selling side. Having the business organized in this fashion meant that Munros' fleet of tippers could be run under 'C' carriers' licences which didn't fall under the controls of nationalized road haulage.

Anyone who has been involved in lime-quarrying work will be aware what a hard and demanding product it is to handle. It was thus somewhat of a relief to hear that the newly elected Conservative Government were to begin denationalizing the long-distance road-haulage structure from about 1953. Young Duncan – then in his mid 20s –

Affectionately known as 'Curly' – because he never had a hair on his head – John Anderson is pictured behind the wheel of his well liked AEC Mercury which dates from 1958. The demountable container was the first one Munros built to try the idea out. With no motorized refrigeration unit, it had four 'whirlies' fitted to the roof: they spun in the air flow, when the vehicle was being driven, to ventilate the inside of the container.

Photographer Roger Kenney spotted Davy Watson at the helm of his 1960 AEC Mammoth Major, one of a number of Mark Vs in the Munro fleet. Others included LRG 798, NRS 86, ORG 311, PRS 665, PRS 765, TRG 52, TRG 719 and TRS 549. Watson is carrying 17 tons of steel plate from Ravenscraig on this occasion, but it was company policy that even an empty vehicle had to be kept sheeted. This kept the platform clean and dry for the paper traffic, and drivers knew that if the old man caught them without their 'skin' on, they would be out of the door.

Although the Clydesdale was really intended to pull only 20 tons when used in articulated form, Munros, like many other hauliers, worked these Albions hard, right up to the maximum permitted 24 tons gross on four axles. PRG 376 is seen coupled to a Crane Fruehauf tandem-axle semi-trailer in this Roger Kenney photograph. The tractor, which dates from 1960, was one of half-a-dozen similar units, its sister Albion, fleet number 112, being registered PRG 374. Two of these Clydesdales had the Leyland 400 engine, the rest had the 375.

was keen to leave the dusty lime of Keith behind but naturally he sought his father's advice about buying up some of the ex-BRS vehicles that were being put up for tender.

'You're in charge of the company,' his father told him, 'if you think you can make a success of it, then do so.'

That was all the encouragement he needed, and by 1956 the dormant company of Munros Transport (Aberdeen) Ltd was raked back into life and the acquisition of ex-BRS vehicles and licences made a fleet that was 13 strong. True, the age and condition of some of the vehicles was questionable, as Jock Smith – current Transport Manager at Munros – recalls: he started driving for the company in that year. Jock's first vehicle was SO 9177, a Perkins P6-engined Albion four-wheeler. King of the road at Munros then was DSC 7, a rather old and weathered ERF. Being an eight-wheeler it could carry almost twice the weight the little Albion could.

For covering local operations, Munros had bought the fleet of eight vehicles of Geordie Scott, based at Alford, but unashamedly Duncan junior much preferred to be involved with long-distance work. A significant early purchase in 1955 for that side of the fleet was to be a quartet of AECs, a marque that was well respected and being bought by anyone who could get their hands on them. Munros sensed that this avenue should be explored further and, after suitable negotiations, the Aberdeen agency for AEC was procured for W.D. Munro Ltd, an involvement with Southall which lasted until 1970 when Leyland finally restructured all the old-established AEC outlets. It should be explained that being an agent for AEC didn't mean that Munros actually sold new vehicles. AEC organized their own travelling sales reps at this time but Munros were to be responsible for repairs, maintenance and the all-important supply of spares.

This facet of the business was embraced under the title of W.D. Munro Ltd Motor Engineers – an all-encompassing term which later saw the company build and make their own pioneering use of demountable refrigerated containers for the carriage of Scottish meat to all parts of the UK mainland. That long-standing class of traffic, lasting until 1982, was still in its infancy in the late 1950s, but what Munros were already well into was the carriage of paper. It's sometimes forgotten that whilst Aberdeen may be currently the centre of North Sea oil activity as well as an old-established supplier of fish, the paper mills adjacent to the River Don are also a big industry in their own right. Carrying pulp or reels to outlets up and down the land was to be a Munro priority.

But even with the latest big AECs, it was a lengthy business. Loading up with paper the previous afternoon, the driver would leave Aberdeen in the early morning and his first day's haul saw him reach Crawford on the A74, which is roughly mid-way between Glasgow and Carlisle. Day two was a good run over the Pennines to reach the Red House at Doncaster and the third day took the much-travelled AEC down to South Mimms. It was only on day four that the driver ran into London and dropped his precious load of paper at its respective customer.

Being 550 miles from base, a back load was essential, and to co-ordinate this class of traffic, Munros, together with Russells of Bathgate, Pollocks of Musselburgh, and Dalkeith Transport & Storage, created in 1959 the London-based company of Express Carriers Ltd. Although they have usually run a couple of vehicles in their own livery as well, Express was created mainly to provide back loads to Scotland for all four partners. The passage of time was to see Russells and Dalkeith drop out from this arrangement, so currently Munros and Pollock share the northbound loads between them.

Long before many of the modern big names in Scottish fridge freight had opted into this specialist line of haulage, Munros were at work using six refrigerated boxes that they manufactured in house. The traffic was mostly meat and they always steered clear of fish. Tommy Sutherland was the regular driver of this 1962 Albion Reiver. Munro men remember it for the way the brakes used to scare the living daylights out of them. They will also tell you how they used to load these Reivers by running up a plank into the box carrying a side of beef over their shoulder.

Establishing bases elsewhere in the early 1960s, Munros began by renting offices in Cheapside Street, Glasgow, at the premises of Maclaren Carriers Agency Ltd. Maclarens, however, went into decline so Munros acquired the former BRS depot at Whitfield Road, primarily to serve the west-central Scotland area. The chain of depots was to be completed in 1964 when a Manchester base was established at Salford, replaced in 1974 by one in Moston.

The Munros yellow-liveried fleet of the 1960s was a classic sight for transport followers. All manner of multi-wheeled artics, eight-, six- and even four-wheeled rigids were used for trunk and tramp operations, so they could be seen in all parts of both Scotland and England. Whilst naturally there was a noticeable bias towards AECs, the Atkinson artic and the Albion Reiver six-wheeled rigids were also used in large numbers. Quickest across the ground was still the AEC, with drivers like Jock Smith saying that the AEC Mercury four-wheeler was probably the finest and fittest vehicle of the time.

The eventual total absorption of AEC by Leyland was not a happy phase for many hauliers, including Munros. Obviously their agency of the marque was lost in 1970, but also lost were the sales of AEC vehicles as Munros began to invest mainly in Atkinsons but also a few Guy Big Js and then ERFs. Another new arrival to the company in 1969 was the third William Duncan Munro who, following his father and grandfather, started straight from school on a five-year apprenticeship as a diesel mechanic.

One bonus with the vehicles that Duncan (WDM 3) found himself working on was that Munros were known as a 'clean fleet'. The decision never to do any form of fresh-fish traffic was taken because of the drawbacks involved with such cargo. Keeping up with the schedule of a roaming fishing fleet must have been bad enough, but what was worse was the way the fish tainted everything it came into

contact with. Munros couldn't have offered a good paper service on a vehicle that may have carried fish, for no matter how often you may have washed the vehicle, the wagon body would carry traces of fish for life. But even that decision wasn't enough for Munros: they had it as company policy that a vehicle's body was always to be sheeted – whether it was loaded or not – so that it was an ideal dry platform for its next consignment of new paper.

Breaking fresh boundaries in 1970 was the much-travelled Jock Smith. It was he who took the accolade of being the first driver from north-east Scotland to run to the Continent with refrigerated freight in a 40ft articulated outfit. This was to be the first of many runs, as the next 12 years saw Munro drivers travel to France, Holland, Belgium and Luxembourg carrying Scottish meat exports into Europe. Closer to home, in 1971, Munros bought the Banff-based haulage concern of Davidsons Transport. Its fleet of three AEC Mandator artics were run from the Moray Coast base for about a year before they were brought across and amalgamated into the Aberdeen fleet. With the end of the AEC agency work, a reassessment of building usage saw a major warehousing construction programme take place in 1974. Storage totalling 20,000 square feet was created, plus other buildings which were to form the basis of Munros current 80,000 square feet of capacity.

Long-established they may have been, with a widely varied customer base, but Munros still found themselves a casualty of the recessional effects in the early 1980s. By 1984, the road fleet had dropped to just above the 40 mark from a mid-1970s peak of close to 100. A total reappraisal of the company's facilities, capital equipment, strategy, planning and marketing was undertaken by the board of four directors, which comprised W.D. Munro senior (WDM 2), W.M. Rennie (Finance), W.D. Munro junior (WDM 3) and G.T. Andrews.

URG 456 made the front page of *Motor Transport* on April 19, 1963, because it was one of five similar tractor units ordered for the Munro fleet, the others being URG 60, URG 750, URS 29 and VRS 753. Reginald Montgomery was the first driver of this Atkinson and Doug Wilcox later drove it for some time. The stylish look of the new wagons didn't cut much ice with the drivers: they called them 'right useless poultices' and found the lack of power from the Gardner 150 engine left them with a sore leg every night.

Moving large consignments of paper has been a Munro hallmark for more than 35 years. Not usually a sign of theirs, though, was the silver rampant horse on the AEC radiator grille in this photograph. The symbol was affixed to every vehicle in another Aberdeen fleet, that of James G. Barrack, but Stanley Ewen, regular driver of this Mandator, liked it so much he acquired one for himself. The Mandators were bought regularly until Munros' AEC agency was discontinued in 1970.

Jock Smith is seen on Fraserburgh Promenade in 1971 having just collected his new refrigerated container from Gray & Adams in the town. Jock regularly left Aberdeen at lunchtime on Saturday in his Rolls-powered Atkinson to deliver meat to Smithfield market in London on Sunday night. Keeping the fresh meat at a controlled temperature of two degrees was a gas-operated Petter fridge unit. What Jock most remembered about this outfit was the back loads from Hayes up to Edinburgh and Montrose. Thousands of boxes of Callard & Bowser sweets were handballed into the container, giving Jock back trouble he has had to live with ever since.

It's sometimes rather painful to take a close look at yourself but valuable too, and the last seven years have seen a complete change-round in the fortunes of Munros. The foundations of local distribution were laid in 1985 when a contract was negotiated with Spillers Milling Flour for the complete Scottish distribution of their products through both the Aberdeen and Glasgow depots. An entirely new line of work was won in late 1987 when a dedicated oil distribution depot was established at Altens in Aberdeen, following negotiations with the Elbar Group for the assets of Elbar Oils. This transaction saw most of the former Elbar Oil staff and vehicles transfer to Munros, and for the first time in the company history they were to operate rigid tankers. A Ford Cargo was the pioneer in this game but that was found to be too small and was replaced by a second-hand Leyland Bison six-wheeler. This in turn was augmented by a Leyland Constructor 6 tanker.

So after a gap of almost 17 years, Leyland Group vehicles were again being bought by Munros. In fact, from 1979 the company had completely stopped buying UK-origin trucks, with Mercedes and MAN being firm favourites. However, with the imports found to be expensive on the spares side, and the need for a simple, no-frills trunk machine being evident, seven Leyland Roadtrains arrived, fitted with the 320 Cummins engine specifically for trunk use.

But it was in distribution, not trunk work, where Munros were principally to expand. In March 1988, the Govan depot was sold and the company moved the Glasgow area of operations to a new 1.5-acre site at East Kilbride. New work coming here was to be the entire distribution of the products of the old-established Glasgow oil company of Percy & Halden, who had sold out to Carless Lubricants. Munros purchased the two-vehicle P & H fleet, a Volvo FL6 and a Fiat. These were the first Iveco vehicle ever in the Munro fleet and the first Volvo for about 10 years, their last Volvo F86 being ORS 754M.

Also in 1989, the West Kilbride carrier company of A. Mc.Jack became available. Munros bought the vehicle assets and became the owners of two rather old Leyland Boxers. Whilst their two carrier runs were merged into one and covered by a new Leyland Freighter, one of the Boxers, ASD 809T, was scrapped, the other one, FGE 565X, being transferred to Aberdeen and painted in Munro colours for use in local north-east work.

All the fleet vehicles were adopting an entirely new livery at this period. The strong yellow of old was going in favour of a distribution white, although the wheeled-M logo was still retained. This new paint scheme was found on a Foden bought specifically to run on the regular trunk service between Aberdeen and Manchester. Fitted with the Caterpillar engine, this sole Sandbach product has quickly

Atkinsons were always to feature strongly in the Munro line-up as they gave the haulier very good service. RSA 609R was put on the road in March 1977 and is seen here 14 years later, in February 1991, in the Aberdeen depot. It now has rather modest shunting duties to perform, but it was first used on demanding trunk work before a lengthy stay at the Glasgow depot. Abbey Farquhar is fastening up a curtainsider which is now almost the standard Munro semi-trailer.

Gordon Andrews was instrumental in bringing back the Leyland tractive unit into the Munro fold after a gap of almost 17 years. He also changed the livery to the current white, retaining the wheeled-M logo for continuity. D452 WSS went on the road on February 5, 1987 and, like its seven counterparts, was used on extensive trunk operations. The Roadtrains all have the Cummins 320 engine, matched to a variety of Spicer and Fuller gearboxes.

proved to be a driver's favourite because of the way it can out-pull anything else on the road.

Changes were also ahead for the Board as Duncan Munro senior retired from being Managing Director, although continuing as Company Chairman. Also retiring at the end of 1989 was Bill Rennie, the Finance Director, who was replaced by Gary Mitchell. This team had done the groundwork for yet further Munro development which was finalized on February 9, 1990. Sometimes, it seems, things can go full circle.

In 1979, Munros' Glasgow depot Manager Bill Mutch had left the company employ to return to the Grampian region as Managing Director of Maclennans Transport of Aberchirder. This concern was a subsidiary of North Eastern Farmers, with whom Munros had been involved in the joint venture of lime quarrying in 1949. North Eastern Farmers were going through a process of rationalization and this culminated in their selling Maclennans Transport to Munros in 1990. Rather than simply absorb Maclennans, the decision was taken to keep it independent but also put massive investment into it. From the 12 vehicles and 16 staff they inherited, Maclennans now have a high profile fleet including five new DAF 95-350 units, a Strato 365 and 18 new Tautliners.

It is Seddon Atkinson which are now numerically strongest in the Munro fleet. Their latest Strato 365 was bought on January 1, 1991 and registered H146 URS, regularly running to Southampton or Portsmouth twice a week. The oldest Atky is a weathered Borderer bought on February 1, 1975 and registered HRS 863N: not having any form of power assistance, it proves hard work for the driver even when just being shunted round the yard. Munros were also to purchase the last batch of Leyland Roadtrains that

were produced, one of which was the last off the production line. Another was sent to Eindhoven and used to develop the new Leyland DAF 80-series. Munros were also the first company to order an 80-series Leyland DAF and received the first vehicle off the production line, albeit not the first registered example. Both will have brass plates fitted to commemorate these facts.

Fitted with a plaque of a different kind, commemorating other changes, is a recently bought second-hand AEC Marshal which is destined for use in distribution work out of the Aberdeen depot. The plate on the driver's door inside the cab advises the reader to contact W.D. Munro Ltd for any service when in the Aberdeen area. And men, like vehicles, also deserve a mention in the Munro story. Ray Smith, who retired in 1990, ran on the Aberdeen to Manchester trunk for almost 30 years and clocked over 2 million miles in that time. Covering slightly less distance but of no less importance was Willie Johnstone (nicknamed Oily Willie), who retired after driving a delivery vehicle for an oil customer for exactly 30 years.

Munros have certainly changed in more ways than one since 1933: in fact the latest concern of theirs, St Machar's Storage Services, is to run five new vehicles which won't even have Munros' name on them at all. Working for the Donside Paper Company, the new vehicles are painted in a mixture of Cornflower Blue and Aircraft Blue, hauling curtainsider semi-trailers. What gives these vehicles away is the smallest part of the signwriting on the cab doors, for if you look closely, you will find some strange names, 'Beinn Lutharn Mhor', 'Carn an Righ', 'Carn an Fhidleir', 'An Socach' and 'Carn Aosda', which, as anyone interested in fell-walking or mountaineering will tell you, are five of the Grampian Munros.

Opposite: Maclennans are now a wholly owned subsidiary of the Munro organization, the parent's early influences showing in a new buying policy of Sed Atki Strato and Leyland DAF 95 vehicles all with similar cabs. Exemplifying the latest 26-pallet curtainsider, this Montracon semi-trailer chassis with Boalloy top delivers North Eastern Farmers' Grampian Oat Products nationally from the New Oatmeal Mill at Boyndie near Banff. H387 TSA, new on October 1, 1990, is regularly driven by Bruce Durno, known for his Iveco Ford jacket which he goes on wearing in the hope that Seddon Atkinson will replace it with a new one of theirs!

Fleet list

Munros Transport (Aberdeen) Ltd

Rigids

Reg no	Make/type
A616 DSS	Mercedes-Benz
B137 LSS	MAN
MLK 745V	Ford
MSR 385Y	Ford
B338 LRS	Mercedes-Benz
YRS 573Y	Mercedes-Benz
UMW 931T	Leyland Bison*
XSO 618Y	Mercedes-Benz
TMS 769X	Leyland
F178 GSS	Leyland DAF
A443 OYC	DAF 2100
FGE 565X	Leyland
NGG 641Y	Volvo
B505 EAM	Leyland Constructor*
B730 NRS	Fiat Ducatto van
G597 PSS	Leyland DAF Freighter
B722 UAS	Ford Cargo 1617
ATS 179V	Land-Rover
KDF 146E	AEC Marshal

[*tanker]

Artic tractor units

Reg no	Make/type	Reg no	Make/type
HRS 863N	Atkinson	G586 PSS	Seddon Atkinson
RSA 609R	Seddon Atkinson	B425 KSA	DAF FTG DKX 6x2
USA 309S	ERF	A793 ESS	DAF FTG DKX 6x2
ASA 613T	ERF	D450 WSS	Leyland Roadtrain
ASA 616T	ERF	D451 WSS	Leyland Roadtrain
FRS 870V	ERF	D452 WSS	Leyland Roadtrain
FSS 999V	ERF	D453 WSS	Leyland Roadtrain
LSS 373W	Seddon Atkinson	D454 WSS	Leyland Roadtrain
XSS 747Y	Mercedes-Benz	D455 WSS	Leyland Roadtrain
YSA 549Y	Mercedes-Benz	D941 XSA	Leyland Roadtrain
YSO 909Y	Mercedes-Benz	G779 EDC	Leyland Roadtrain
YRS 575Y	Mercedes-Benz	G780 EDC	Leyland Roadtrain
XRS 815Y	MAN	G781 EDC	Leyland Roadtrain
B747 LSO	Mercedes-Benz	G783 EDC	Leyland Roadtrain
B617 MSA	MAN	H564 USS	Leyland Roadtrain
A969 GSS	MAN		
XRS 131Y	Mercedes-Benz		
F551 RRF	Foden S10L		
G988 MSS	Leyland Roadtrain		
G989 MSS	Leyland Roadtrain		

Munros mountain names

Munro no	Height*	Gaelic name	English translation
145	994	Carn an Fhidleir	Hill of the Fiddler
85	1,045	Beinn Lutharn Mhor	Big Hill of Hell
98	1,029	Carn an Righ	Hill of the King
221	994	An Socach	Projecting Place
270	917	Carn Aosda	Hill of Age

[*heights in metres]

Fleet list

Maclennans Transport Ltd

Artic tractor units

Reg no	Make/type	Reg no	Make/type
B554 USR	Renault R310 6x2	G375 PRS	Leyland DAF 95-350 4x2
B774 USR	Renault R310 6x2	H91 SRS	Leyland DAF 95-350 4x2
C332 AES	Renault G290 6x2	H92 SRS	Leyland DAF 95-350 4x2
D861 VSO	Renault G290 6x2	H93 SRS	Leyland DAF 95-350 4x2
D740 RHR	MAN 20.331	H387 TSA	Seddon Atkinson Strato
E624 BRS	Iveco 190.36 6x2	H146 URS	Seddon Atkinson Strato
E625 BRS	Iveco 190.36 6x2	F168 HSS	Iveco 190-36 Turbostar
F816 PSE	DAF FT 95-350 4x2		
F817 PSE	DAF FT 95-350 4x2	**Pick-up**	
F818 PSE	DAF FT 95-350 4x2		
G412 OSS	Leyland DAF RT 17-32	A211 MKO	Ford Transit
G374 PRS	Leyland DAF 95-350 4x2		

2: Richard Preston & Son Ltd and FVS Ltd

If you examine a map of England, even one with a large scale, you will be hard pushed to find mention of a place called Potto. But drive down the A1, day or night, and look out for some well turned-out red-coloured Seddon Atkinson, Volvo, DAF or ERF outfits and it won't be long before you will find this place name closely connected to the haulage concern of Prestons. Together with sister company FVS Ltd, Prestons of Potto is the banner which flies over 170 vehicles, 400 trailers, 30 acres of development, 300,000 square feet of warehousing and a staff 250 strong based at three main depots. Involved in all manner of haulage, distribution and warehouse management, Richard and Anne Preston are at the helm of a company which continues to provide positive proof that 'big business' and 'family business' are not mutually exclusive terms. A big champion of the Road Haulage Association, Prestons also strive to create one of the finest images in the business, not only with their premium fleet but also with the head office at Potto, arguably one of the most impressive HQs in the industry.

Potto is, in fact, a peaceful and tranquil North Yorkshire village situated about three miles east of the A19 trunk road and about the same distance south of the boundary of the heavily industrialized county of Cleveland. An obscure place as the centre of one of the largest general hauliers in the area it may be, but it was simply the fact that Prestons were at Potto that brought them into the haulage business mostly by accident in 1957. This line of work was a big turn-round from the agricultural business that Prestons were heavily involved in at that time, and to trace its beginnings we must look back to 1936. It all started then because a farmer missed his market for corn because his brother was rather unreliable.

That farmer was one William Percy Thomas, who farmed at Seamer Moor. He needed his brother, William Henry Thomas, who also farmed, at Langbaurgh Grange Farm, Great Ayton and carried out a threshing business

from there, to come and thresh his corn for him. Richard Preston senior was a driver for William Henry and was sent to Seamer Moor to thresh William Percy's corn. But there had been some delay and the latter was so annoyed about missing the best market for his grain that he vowed to go into the threshing business himself. Richard senior was asked if he would like to go into partnership with him and in that way Preston & Thomas, threshing contractors, was established. Mr Thomas was to die within six months of this concern being set up: in time, Preston bought out the shares left to Mrs Thomas and the concern was his alone.

The late 1930s and early '40s were a busy time for Preston, for the wartime years meant all available land going under the plough to produce food. Timber cutting became another Preston wartime effort and for two years a sawmill was operated near Doncaster, with six saw benches driven by two steam engines doing work exclusively for the National Coal Board.

At this time, Preston had about six engines, but during the late 1940s there was a decline in threshing and contracting work and Preston sensed it was time for a change. A big investment saw him go into grass and grain drying. A large shed was built at Potto, at a cost of £750, and the milling equipment inside was to cost a further £20,000. Fortunately, a contract was obtained from the Ministry of Agriculture which kept the machinery going for two years, operating 24 hours a day, seven days a week. When that contract ended, Preston at first did drying work for others in the area but as most farmers began to invest in their own drying equipment, he switched his men to cable laying for the GPO using Marshall tractors. They also undertook dressing grain for seed, continued woodsawing, and of course retained one of the steamers, normally all fired up, for steam cleaning purposes.

It was this traditional mode of traction which caught the eye of a man passing through Potto station on his way to

Once retired, 'Lightning II' was restored to all its former glory and is pictured at its first steam rally at Levens Hall near Kendal in 1959. The Burrell three-speed road locomotive, apparently the only one ever to leave the factory painted green, was first run by the showman partnership Emmerson & Hazard of Barrow-in-Furness. It was sold to Prestons in 1956 and is still ritually steamed every year across country to Masham, stopping en route at Brompton for water. Accompanying it here is the late Richard Preston senior, naturally proud of his engine – and his figure.

work and in so doing changed the whole path of Preston's business. That man was a director of Crossleys, a local brick manufacturer, and in 1957 his company was suffering the effects of the Suez crisis. With a shortage of fuel causing them to lay vehicles up, the steamer seemed an ideal alternative that didn't use diesel.

'Will it haul bricks?' he pointedly asked Preston senior, and without hesitation the reply was 'Yes'.

I doubt if Richard Preston senior knew what he was letting himself in for. What he got was the contract to haul all the bricks that Crossleys were producing at their Hurworth plant for a major contract to extend the famous Ampleforth College. So, with two trailers hung on behind 'Lightning II', Preston senior, accompanied by fireman Kit Walls and trailer brake man Jack Pearson, clanked over to Hurworth, near Darlington for his first 25 tons of bricks.

This was the start of three months of very hard graft. It was a good day's work to journey down to Ampleforth, which is mid-way between Thirsk and Pickering, but it was the tight country lanes around Coxwold that really made the Preston team earn their money. A second day was spent handballing the bricks from the trailers and then running back empty to load up yet again. The only saving grace for Preston was that Crossleys had just invested in some new fork-lifts so at least they didn't have to load the bricks on by hand.

Richard Preston senior was two stones lighter by the time the Ampleforth work was finished. By then, diesel fuel was in more regular supply and 'Lightning' could at last be laid up. Thankfully this particular exercise in haulage wasn't to be repeated, but the experience had given Preston both an insight and a toe-hold into the road transport world. For his first conventional vehicle Richard Preston went to Chambers & Holliday who had the Thornycroft agency in Garden Street, Darlington. A Sturdy four-wheeler was bought and, running up to 14 tons gross, it was worked

PPY 618M was Prestons' first specialized bulk hauler, built by Murfitt of Wisbech to handle granule traffic. Loaded via a system of top hatches, the cargo was kept clean by a new plastic liner inserted into the tipping semi-trailer before each load was taken on. This photograph was taken at ICI's massive Marske complex.

under contract 'A' licence first, also on brick haulage.

Prestons had, in fact, run a Thornycroft four-wheeler many years earlier. Their sole wagon had been driven by Richard junior on straw delivery but the vehicle had been sold once he had gone into the RAF for his National Service. The passage of time evidently hadn't much improved this marque, as Prestons were soon to brand the second Thornycroft 'an implement of torture'. The poor performance of the vacuum-hydraulic brakes meant that the bottom sections of steep hills like Sutton Bank were done with little form of retardation and the driver in a permanent state of prayer. Equally sharply recalled was the descent of Sawley Brow near Clitheroe which was encountered on the regular run with grain down to Liverpool. Even with the handbrake fully ratcheted back, Preston junior says his back seemed in a perpetual arch as he strained to exert maximum pressure on the brake pedal. Thankfully, an AEC Mercury, WVN 89, was eventually to replace the Thornycroft, the stopping power of air brakes being a positive luxury in comparison.

In the infancy of their career as hauliers, Prestons soon proved themselves quick learners. They were to join the

Road Haulage Association as early as July 1957 and getting involved with that membership proved to be of invaluable help. Finding their feet, they looked round to see what other hauliers in the area were using as work-horses and took the example of the well respected hauliers Sandersons of Great Broughton for guidance. Sandersons had put their faith in the Atkinson chassis, with Gardner engine, David Brown gearbox, Kirkstall axle and Michelin tyres, a combination that Prestons too were to adopt. The fact that there are still a couple of old Atky Borderers used as shunters at Potto gives some indication of how reliable a combination this has been.

Of more questionable performance was a Dodge six-wheeler that Prestons bought second-hand primarily for its carriers' licence, converting it from a tipper to a platform for general haulage use. Under its bonnet was a Cummins V6 engine and, in true tipper fashion, it did its best to create as much smoke and noise as possible. For this, Prestons were to feel the wrath of the Metropolitan Police and were duly summoned to attend Willesden Magistrates' Court. Although the smoke and noise output were slightly high, Prestons felt aggrieved and, after taking RHA advice, they consulted Mr Campbell-Wardlaw, reputedly the best brief in the land at that time when it came to goods-vehicle matters. He agreed to defend them and, appearing before the Bench, his way with words created enough doubt in the Magistrates' minds to prompt them to dismiss the charges.

Encouraged to visit a nearby hostelry to celebrate the fact that justice had been done, Richard Preston was still in awe of the great man's oratory and asked him how he had done it. 'Mr Preston junior,' – he was the only man who ever referred to Richard in that fashion – 'you should always remember that the Magistrates like to hear a story. But never forget that you've got to make them feel important – important enough to make them believe your side of the story.'

The most significant things to happen in the Preston story during the 1960s were not things that seemed to have any immediate effect on matters but which in the long run were to prove exceptionally important. It was in 1960 that the last railway train ran along the branch line through Potto station. About half a mile from Potto village itself, this small piece of industrialized land may not have ranked high on many people's shopping list. But it was just across the road from the Preston house and base, and purchase of this land assured the accommodation for any foreseeable

This gathering of staff at Potto in 1975 was to commemorate the occasion when Prestons flew the flag and went into Europe for the first time. Without appropriate permits, they were limited to travelling no more than 25 kilometres from the landing port, Calais. The F88 Volvos were fully laden with granules for use in the manufacture of cables. Just sneaking into shot is ARC 969B, a 9.6-litre AEC Mammoth Major which launched Prestons into the big time after it was bought second-hand from Tony Walker. It was still in use as a wrecker at this later stage.

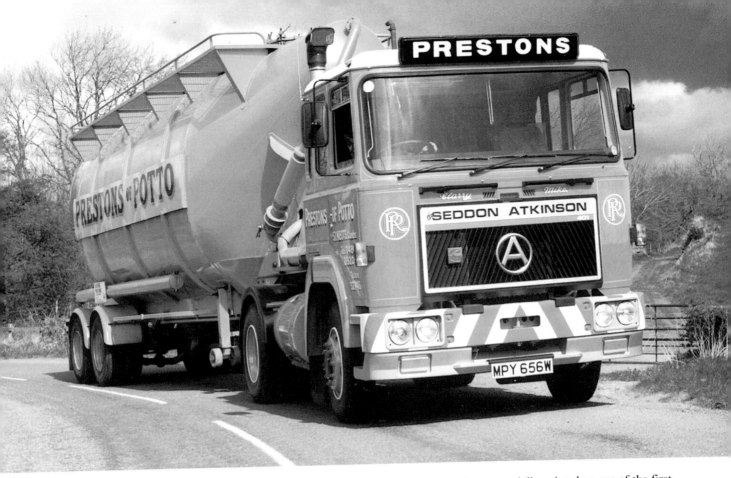

You won't find many of the Preston vehicles carrying individual names but 'Clarry' and 'Mike' were specially painted on one of the first Seddon Atkinson 401 Cummins 290 tractors to come into the area. Potto-based trunker Clarry Arston and St Neots shunter Mike Mortimer have been working a double act for more years than people care to remember. Seen near Potto when new in 1980, the vehicle ran up to 32 tons gross with this Murfitt-based tank semi-trailer.

Preston expansion. In hindsight, what was a rail-network loss was very much a Preston gain, as the current base at Potto now embraces all the old station real estate with only the odd preserved BR sign indicating what existed just over 30 years ago.

In that same year of 1960, Richard Preston was to marry Anne and in 1965 she decided to join forces with him in their fledgling transport concern. Anne, by then the mother of youngsters David and Jayne Preston, was no stranger to road haulage. She had often travelled with her father who ran an AEC Mercury hauling cattle, milk and even passengers from their North Cowton base, with Darlington Market being a regular port of call. She had qualified to take up top secretarial posts but, after some extended maternity leave, it was to be the Preston transport business where all her efforts were targeted. In 1969, Richard Preston and Son Ltd became the newly incorporated title of that business. With the company bearing the name of his father, Richard junior and his wife Anne were given charge to build on the 12 years of foundations, and the 1970s saw them out on the acquisition trail.

Although the changes created in the 1968 Transport Act had ended the need for buying and selling 'A' carriers' licences, in certain other respects contracts still had to be bought if you wanted to get into a specific field. Although Prestons had carried some steel from Skinningrove as an

early diversification from their brick and grain traffic, getting access into the main Teesside steel works proved more difficult. Most of the steel was moved by a fixed number of contactors, but after buying up the interests of firstly C.W. Tinklers and then FVS Ltd, Prestons were to get the key to this select market.

FVS – Freeman, Volkers and Stuart – had been one of the first hauliers to run contracts from the Teesside steel works but by 1972 their operations, working out of Phoenix Sidings in Stockton, had been run down. The FVS buy-out was to encompass the steel contracts, four artic tractor units – a Guy and three Atkinsons – plus five semi-trailers. At the last minute, a sixth semi-trailer was included in the sale and although not of great financial importance that same trailer still rates a soft spot in the Preston memoirs. Designated 'FVS trailer No 1', it is a 33ft-long Walker-built coil carrier of such well made yet light design it still works day in and day out, its big boon being that it never overloads its axles no matter where the coils are dropped in.

Initially, the FVS wagons were transferred to the Tinkler yard which was in Station Road at Norton, but this wasn't very satisfactory. Being located in a residential area was bad enough, but getting access into the ex-Tinkler workshops was almost comical. As tractor units had steadily grown in size they had in fact outgrown the height of the Station Road workshop doors: the only way to get a vehicle inside

Above: With the announcement of the 38-tonne legislation, Prestons converted their trailer fleet to tri-axles, mostly by sending them back to their original manufacturers for uprating. Hauling at the new weight limit, BPY 618Y was one of six ERF 'C' types that arrived together, this one having the Cummins 290 engine. The load is being carried on a standard Crane Fruehauf 40ft semi-trailer. The driver is Billy Carling from Ripon. Prestons bought out a number of smaller operations, but they retained the name, livery and separate identity of Freeman, Volkers and Stuart Ltd rather than absorbing it totally. Ken Monaghan is the face behind the wheel of PPY 678X, one of the last 'B' series ERFs taken into service by the group. The Cummins-powered tractor is coupled to a Crane Fruehauf semi-trailer, carrying a 20-tonne vessel on Teesside.

was first to take off the two front wheels and then run it in on its brake drums! With practical difficulties like this it wasn't surprising that Prestons were happy to acknowledge the local Council's observations that a growing haulage operation wasn't really compatible with the wishes of the nearby residents. Fortunately, the time coincided with Pickfords closing down their depot in Church Road at Stockton so once again a nationalized concern's loss was a Preston gain. This depot had in fact started its transport life before World War 2 when Fred Robinson had it specially built for his expanding fleet, only to see it all compulsorily acquired during nationalization in 1949. Firstly run by BRS, it was passed to Pickfords heavy haulage, and then tankers and furniture vans used it until the early 1970s.

With outward-bound traffic from the North-East now firmly established, Prestons found there was a growing customer demand for a southern distribution network. Obviously this couldn't be done from Potto, so in search of somewhere suitable, Richard and Anne drove down to London to look for themselves. Working back up the A1 they visited every estate agent dealing with the type of

commercial property that they were after, but without any success. By the time they got to St Neots they felt that if they didn't find somewhere soon it wouldn't be worth their while as they would be too far north of the capital. In desperation they went to the local council only to learn that their trading estate was full – but they were just in the process of finishing a new one at Eaton Socon so Prestons were offered the pick of the plots. That southern office, workshop, and refuelling depot has since expanded, with three further adjacent plots being taken up by Preston for use as warehousing, and is now home for about 20 southern-based vehicles. The big advantage of St Neots is that, no matter how the drivers' hours regulations have fluctuated in the last 20 years or so, the relatively good standard of the A1 has allowed for a return round-trip between the HQ at Potto and the St Neots depot in a single day/night's trunk.

The framework which the Prestons established in the early 1970s has been the basis of their big expansion. Undoubtedly it has been the FVS side of operations, always referred to as Anne's baby, that has undergone the biggest

Probably the only truck to have been featured in the society magazine *The Tatler*, Prestons' 25th Wedding Anniversary special created a lot of excitement when it first appeared in 1985. Seen outside the magnificent head office at Potto, the Spacecab DAF 3300 Murfitt 38-tonner was first entrusted to driver Mick Rowles who is the longest-serving employee with the company. It was later repainted in the livery of British Steel and is now regularly driven by Steve Neasham. Right, Billy Carling again, this time in 1985 with what for him is quite a modest load of steel beams out of the BSC Lackenby plant on Teesside. Carrying the weight is a Broshuis trombone-type semi-trailer whose tri-axles are on steel suspension. Billy is recognized as the King Pin at Prestons when it comes to long steel and 80ft lengths are routine to him. His DAF 3300 A77 FDC has a twin sister, A76 FDC . Billy now pilots an MAN tractor unit which arrived in late 1989 as a seed vehicle and was bought by Prestons for long-term evaluation. Early reactions are favourable. Below right, F70 SAJ is affectionately referred to as 50% of the FVS heavy-haulage division, the other half being Mercedes-Benz G841 DPY. In this 1990 photograph, driver Alan Camp is following police escort instructions to take to the grass with an extremely awkward fabrication which gave the outfit an overall length close to 125ft. It was one of six similar loads constructed by Redpath Engineering in Stockton for the bridge being built over the Thames at Dartford. Supported on a Broshuis trailer hired from Hudsons of Bawtry, the load has just left Norblast, where it had been shotblasted and painted, via the Black Path.

Although specializing in steel transportation, FVS will of course carry any form of general haulage traffic, especially when back loading. They also handle a lot of deliveries for the local Stockton concern J. B. Smith whose timber yard and joinery works are in Dovedale Street. The FVS wagon pictured having just loaded there is a Mercedes 1633 with EPS transmission, regular driver Ian Marley at the wheel.

In February 1990, Ian Semple of Northern Photographic Services scaled the heights to record this selection of what Prestons use and some of the companies among their clients. The vehicles in Preston livery have window stickers indicating the firm's specialist divisions, food, steel, engineering, industrial and fertilizers. The one 'spoof' is the Foden eight-wheeler, third from left: it was kindly loaned by London Brick for the occasion to reflect the quantity of bricks carried by Prestons. The Foden third from the right is a Preston vehicle, a Cat-powered air-suspended eight-wheeler which works out of the Birtley base of Redland Tiles.

changes. The transformation to an immaculate, high-profile fleet now counted as 50 strong means the FVS operations can compare with any other steel carrier in the land. The name was retained for its association with pioneering steel work, and it is run as a completely separate operation, although there is still a great deal of intermingling with the Preston parent as and when the traffic flow dictates.

Whilst FVS makes steel a speciality, the Preston side of operations is particularly wide in its variety of traffic. Tautliners, tankers, trombones, low-loaders and conventional flats and rigids carry chemicals, steel, building merchants' materials, food, household products, liquids and powders in bulk – in fact it's probably easier to say what Prestons don't do and that is tippers and car transporters. Anything else, Prestons will probably be able to move, a formula that has been reached by a great deal of effort expended by a great number of people. That effort was reflected in Prestons being accredited with the award of a BS5750 quality assurance certificate in 1989, one of the first privately owned transport and warehousing companies to receive that qualification.

The effort hasn't only been channeled into championing the Preston cause, for Anne Preston in particular has shown staunch involvement in the Road Haulage Association. She was the first woman to be a member of the RHA National Council and Chairman of the Long-Distance British Committee and is currently Chairman of the North-Eastern district. In 1987 she was awarded the MBE in recognition of her services to the road haulage industry.

With a track record like that it's not surprising how well known the Preston name is. However, that recognition still cannot enlarge the size of Potto on the map, though you would be amazed at the wide range of activities carried out at this idyllic North Yorkshire road transport base.

3: R. Sinclair (Transport) Ltd

Historically, the Vale of Evesham has often been called the 'Garden of England' and even today it is well known throughout the land for its fruit-growing industry. Less than 50 years ago it also produced all manner of vegetables and hauling this form of produce to all parts of the country was how Evesham-based R. Sinclair Ltd established its roots in the transport world. Managing Director and company founder Ron Sinclair now oversees a solid line-up firmly based on DAF 95-350 traction. Fellow directors are his sons David, Terry, Nigel and Sean who, after starting off as company drivers, now co-ordinate operations of the 24-strong fleet and 35,000 square feet of warehousing at the purpose-built Davies Road base. Outward-bound traffic, which is normally sourced from a 25-mile radius around Evesham, is delivered to all parts of the UK mainland. With the words 'England–Scotland' proudly emblazoned across the front of their blue livery, Sinclairs' 38-tonners deliver as far afield as Dounreay in northern Scotland or Penzance in the deepest south-west. Quite an area for a general haulage operation, especially when you learn that it all started with no more than two tons of cabbages taken no further than an hour's run up the road to Birmingham.

It was in 1947 that 21-year old Ron Sinclair came home to Evesham from military service and, although having little in the way of prospects or money, latched on to an opportunity which not only required a strong nerve but also a strong back. At this period, it was slowly being realized that the virtual stranglehold which the railways had over transport could be eaten into by a willing road haulage system. Speed of delivery was something that road haulage could offer for all manner of traffic, an aspect of service that the railways couldn't always guarantee because of the rigidity and complexities of the system. Getting a vehicle to set up in transport was particularly easy as all manner of wheeled wartime surplus was going under the hammer at ordnance depots all over the place. However, getting a carriers' licence to act as a haulage contractor could be either impossible or just plain extortionate due to the expense involved. What was being given away by the licensing authority was the 'C' licence, although all this allowed you to do was to haul your own goods.

Ron Sinclair put these factors together and, after the issue of a suitable fruit and vegetable licence by the Ministry of Agriculture, went into business as a merchant. In essence, he was a middle man and he would buy produce from the local growers, load it on to his vehicle and then transport it on for delivery to his pre-arranged buyers. The telephone became Ron's lifeline into the business scene and although the first sales and deliveries were made nearby in the Birmingham area, it was to be in Sheffield and the heart of West Yorkshire where Sinclair was to make his mark.

Ron's first load carrier was an American Ford van that had been used by the army as an ambulance. Only rated by the military at 30 cwt (so naturally a 30% overload was in order) it paid for its keep, then was sold on in favour of a left-hand-drive GMC, also petrol driven, but capable of all of five or six tons. Loaded to the gunnels, Ron made his way north where many years of wartime shortages ensured there were ample customers for fresh Evesham produce. Ron recalls that the best contract he won was with the Yorkshire Co-op to service the stores around Morley, Batley, Huddersfield and Heckmondwike.

The Jimmy had cost Ron £320 but it soon paid for itself and, with huge numbers of ex-WD vehicles still available, spare parts, spare engines and even spare vehicles could be easily picked up at your local dealer at little cost. The only thing which wasn't available to Ron was a regular flow of traffic, as his sales were linked to the fairly short growing seasons of the fruit and vegetables involved. When the seasons were made shorter, though, like the bad winter of 1947, the resultant scarcity of produce could sometimes mean an increase in prices, thus profits to the skilful

It was with ex-WD vehicles like th[e] bonneted Dodge four-wheeler that R[on] Sinclair started out in the world [of] transport. Seen in Evesham in about 194[?] it shares the photograph with one of tw[o] 1935 AEC Mammoth Majors bought wh[en] his father joined him in the distributi[on] trade.

merchant. Ron's expertise in the trade soon came to the notice of his father, also called Ron, who had originally been in the mineral-water ('pop') business. Ron senior decided to join in with his son; as well as contributing a stake to buy extra vehicles, the real sweetener to this expansion was a potato licence.

Unlike the fruit and vegetable licence, the authority to buy and sell potatoes was like gold. Ron's brother Jim Sinclair had been seriously injured during the war and as a way of encouraging his rehabilitation the Ministry had given him a potato licence which was now thrown into the expanding Sinclair pot. To haul this new heavyweight cargo the Sinclairs first invested in a pair of maturing six-wheeled AEC Mammoth Minors but these were soon replaced by ex-WD AEC 6x4 units that were the basis of the well known Militant range.

What the wartime years had engendered both in military and civilian life was a way of making do and getting on with things. The camaraderie of a closely knit Sinclair family and Evesham community meant that even though the Sinclair

vehicles were old and weathered, there was always someon[e] who knew the whys and wherefores of keeping the[m] running. Only fitted with 7.7-litre engines, the big si[x] wheelers had their super-single tyres replaced wit[h] conventional twins. To meet the demand for more an[d] more potatoes, a brace of drawbar trailers were bought a[t] £100 a time to increase capacity. Recalled as being a bit o[f] a pig to drive, the big AEC drawbar outfits had a willing i[f] small heart which needed both the driver's hands to get th[e] best from their two-stick transmission.

Into the 1950s, the Sinclair family business wa[s] expanding quickly with about five other men also in full-time employ. But to young Ron, they seemed to be runnin[g] just to stand still. The hard potato work was taking its tol[l] of the AECs in breakdowns and even though replacement[s] were easily available, they too were just the same old ex-WD stuff. There just wasn't the money being made for th[e] big step-up to buying something new, so after a great deal of thought Ron decided that it was time to change tack. His thoughts coincided with an approach from Walter Craft &[...]

On restarting, Ron traded under the name[?] R. Sinclair junior to avoid any confusio[n] with his father who still had transport interests in the Evesham area. UAB 790 was the first Sinclair AEC Mercury, bough[t] new in 1958. Very similar from the front, XWP 435 was the firm's second brand-new AEC, this time a Mustang 'Chinese Six'[.] Two other Mercury four-wheelers that were to come in 1962, registered 87 and 88 JAB, would have the glassfibre cab built by Oswald Tillotson.

or 32-ton artic work, Sinclairs bought a sizeable number of AEC Mandators, though YNP 80G was one of only six of them to have the
8 engine. Pictured in early 1969, the outfit is here in front of the Round House which is nowadays a pedestrian precinct in Evesham town
entre. The face behind the wheel is that of Brian Vann because the wagon's regular driver, Dave Tidmarsh, wasn't available when the
EC photographer came to call. Sinclairs even had to mock up a suitable load for the day: all that is being carried under the sheets is
hree stacks of empty pallets.

Son, a corn merchant from Chipping Norton who also had base at the aptly named Corn Mill Lane in Evesham. They were running two vehicles of their own on corn delivery but were keen for young Ron to buy their vehicles and run them on contract 'C' licences, hauling their dedicated corn and feed traffic. Ron decided to give it a try and for six months he ran their 1948 Bedford 6-tonner before deciding he could make a go of it.

Ron took the second vehicle, a 1949 Thornycroft, in 1952 and for about four years the corn work was his alone, with a part-time driver taken on for about six months every year to drive the Bedford on seasonal work. Describing his Thornycroft Sturdy 7–8 tonner as underpowered, a terrible starter with its indirect-injection engine and awful on the brakes, Ron still felt, for reliability and profit return, it was a lovely little motor.

That generation of profit over four years built Ron a big enough stake to invest in an ex-BRS AEC Monarch four-wheeled dropsider which was bought from John Brindley of Hinckley. With it came the luxury of an 'S' licence, which was a special form of 'A' licence and at last gave the young Sinclair entry into the select brotherhood of long-distance, hire and reward haulage. The first real opening in non-agricultural work was hauling packaged scrap from a metal pressing factory at Stratford-upon-Avon down to a South

Wales steelworks for recycling. Sinclair's first trip coincided with a rail strike so when he asked the Welsh steel men if they had a back load for the Midlands they naturally shook his hand off and in no time there was 10 tons of steel on the back of the little 7.7-powered AEC, destined for Birmingham.

This combination of running loaded into and out of South Wales put Sinclair firmly on his feet. Double-shifting the AEC generated the cash to buy another ex-BRS 'S'-licensed vehicle, this time a Maudslay Mogul, also powered by the AEC 7.7-litre engine. At £2,100 the second-hand four-wheeler wasn't cheap, but really you were paying £1,000 or £1,500 simply for the carriers' licence alone. Ron Sinclair hadn't left his vegetable merchanting business totally behind and, between loads of steel, movements of 'greens' were done as and when required. With his father and other members of the Sinclair family still doing this type of delivery work, Ron worked under the name of R. Sinclair junior, to prevent any confusion, a title that was kept until limited company status was adopted in 1971.

That was to be a big day for Ron, but an even more memorable occasion was when he bought his first brand-new AEC Mercury four-wheeler, UAB 790. It was in early 1958 and Ron paid £2,850 for his latest pride and joy, obviously taking it straight round home to the Sinclair

27

WNP 953M was one of many AEC Mercurys that gave Sinclairs great deal of trouble-free service. Scotsman Tom Currie is driver in this CVRTC photograph, his load being steel pipes whi were of high volume but low weight and came from Speed St of Alcester. Carrying them is a body made by Hawley Mills Walsall, the aluminium frame supporting a wooden bed for ext resilience.

KNP 889N was the prelude to Sinclairs' acceptance of the Vol marque. During comparative trials against the ERF, it return 7.4mpg. The F88 was Sinclairs' first taste of the 290bhp engin coupled to a 16-speed range-change gearbox. Here coupled to Crane semi-trailer, the vehicle is loaded with canned fo destined for delivery in Scotland.

council house for the family to inspect it. Ron's wife Doreen and their four sons climbed aboard to wallow in the luxury of AEC's finest. A 22ft body carried on 10.00 x 20 tyres was capable of a 10-ton load that could be stopped on a sixpence by the latest-specification air brakes. It had taken more than 10 years of hard graft and to Sinclair junior it was one of his finest hours, even though his wife had hoped the money would be spent to buy their own house. When asked what she thought of it, she naturally had mixed feelings and the understandable response when looking round the cab was 'I don't think much of my kitchen.' Ron knew what she meant, so quick as a flash he said, 'Yes, but with this I'll buy you an even better kitchen.'

It was to be a few years before that promise was fulfilled because the next 'new kitchen' Ron bought was an AEC Mustang, XWP 435. This was a 'Chinese Six' which gave Sinclairs a heavier carrying capacity but also their first introduction to the wrath of the Traffic Commissioners. Ron had been able to buy these two new wagons only by

working his ex-BRS machines very hard, but not everyone seemed to appreciate his modest success. Although it wa quite in order to transfer his carrier's licence from the ex-BRS wagons on to the new AECs, it got a bit prickly when you went from a four-wheeler up to a six-legger. At its lightest weight, the Mustang tipped the scales at 5 tons 2 cwt, but all Ron had was a licence for 4 tons 10 cwt. You were allowed a 10 cwt adjustment almost by rubber stamping, thus leaving Ron 2 cwt in the red, but in deciding to take a chance and use the new six-wheeler, he wasn't aware that he would be shopped by an envious competitor. He was hauled before Traffic Commissioner James at Birmingham to be accounted for, but an open admission as to how and why he had transgressed was met with a liberal method of sentencing. 'You don't deserve to be punished,' was the word from Mr James and all Ron had to endure was the grounding of the Mustang for 14 days.

The experience had taught Sinclair a lot. His readings into the fine print of the licensing regulations augured well

KUY 938N was Sinclairs' sole ERF, run for an eight-month trial to assess its potential as a replacement for the long-serving AEC Mandators. Powered by the eight-cylinder Gardner engine and handled by regular driver Don Green, it returned just over 8mpg with a payload of slightly more than 21 tons. It is seen here fitted with extra fuel tanks giving a total capacity of 120 gallons, and coupled to a Crane semi-trailer. The ERF was subsequently sold on to another Evesham firm, Marshalls, and it also appeared in the mid-1980s TV series *Truckers*.

Sinclairs were quite taken with the Ford 'D' series and at one time had about 20 of them in service. Ten were fitted with van bodies, five were used on general haulage, and five were fitted with open slatted bodywork as shown here. The slats gave extra security in transit for boxes of vegetables without an excessive penalty in unladen weight. Don Bennett was the regular driver of RAB 980P, usually working a variety of routes between the Midlands, Nottingham and South Wales areas.

for him until the upheaval of the 1968 Transport Act which ousted the 'A', 'B' and 'C' licences in favour of the easily obtainable 'O'. But by then Sinclair had become a name to be reckoned with as his efforts made their mark in Evesham haulage circles. Like many people before him, Ron had learnt that getting any new licences from the Traffic Commissioners was almost impossible. Getting variations, however, was a little bit easier. So what Sinclair did was to buy up vehicles in the area, as and when they became available, then, armed with the support of good customers, his case was argued in the courts for the licences to be varied to suit the customers' needs. Being able to present a good argument secured some success, prompting an expansion of the fleet, still firmly favouring AEC, but now based out at Badsey.

Obviously, AECs weren't always acquired in the first instance when vehicles and licences were being bought up: Austins, BMCs, Commers, Fords and Leylands came but then went in favour of yet more Mercurys and Mustangs.

With AEC having a depot at West Bromwich and Maudslay's old factory only 8 miles outside Evesham, there were plenty of men in the area who knew how to service or repair this famous Southall marque.

The expanding fleet also saw an expansion in traffic flow. The scrap-metal work from the pressing factory led to cannery traffic from another branch of the same organization. Mining machinery also became regular and, with seasonal fruit and vegetables still being very popular, Sinclair leapt at the chance to go into articulation as a way of increasing the efficiency of his traction. Naturally the AEC Mercury coupled to a four-in-line semi-trailer was adopted as the preferred company combination, for this gave a very light unladen weight allowing for a 17-ton payload within the maximum 24-ton limit. Some of the tractor units had in fact started life as rigid four-wheelers but Sinclairs did their own conversions into artic units as the Mercury proved to be a willing work-horse.

But although it did its best at 24 tons, the Mercury

Sinclairs stayed with Volvos, choosing the F10 as a replacement for the F88 tractor unit. Pictured fully laden with canned foodstuffs outside their Worcester Road base, NUY 54T had John Turner as its regular driver. The F10 gave Sinclairs good service but proved rather expensive if kept for more than about three years. Problems with turbochargers and liner seals began to occur if there was any water loss.

In the mid-1980s, Ron Sinclair opted for the DAF 3300 in preference to the 2800, the extra power making it easier to maintain good journey times. Mac Taylor is now the owner-driver of this 3300, though Sinclairs were its first owner and operator and it still carries their livery. All three vehicles that Mac has had have come from the Sinclair fleet, so naturally he will be first in line for a 95 when they come up for change. The outfit is here loaded with 24 tons of mining equipment from Meco International (formerly Dowty) at Worcester for delivery into Yorkshire.

couldn't work up to the 32-ton limit which came into the transport world in 1965. For the heaviest weight band, Sinclairs bought in the Mandators, first with the 690 engines, then with the 760s and half a dozen with the famous V8s. Ron Sinclair reckons the AEC V8 engine was about 20 years before its time, but one of its failings was the regular breakage of the alloy bell housing. The only way this was combated was by fitting the cast-iron bell housing from the marine version of the same engine. Although the Leyland empire didn't pursue the use of the V8, Sinclairs were also involved with Perkins Engines who carried out trials over two years with a Mandator fitted with a prototype T640 Perkins V8 engine. The eventual intercooled version produced 290bhp, massive power in the

early 1970s, and although it tended to blow head studs off, Sinclair took a lot of pleasure from being in on this experimental work.

Whilst the Mandator was undoubtedly the Sinclair flagship, being given a new AEC was only achieved by seniority and merit. The Sinclair sons who came into the business in the mid-1960s were expected to cut their teeth on the oldest hand-me-downs, which at the time were some lightweight Thames Traders that had been bought to gain their licences. David Sinclair recalls that his Trader's top speed was a modest 48mph. If you pushed it too hard, an injector would go or, if you really hammered it, then a pushrod would snap. Both David and Terry Sinclair always carried a spare pushrod and a No 6 injector pipe, the

Although the fleet now operates predominantly in the 38-tonne range, space limitations at some points of customer access dictate that Sinclairs retain a brace of four-wheelers. This John Simons photograph taken in February 1991 shows John Meadows manoeuvring his DAF 1900 in the Davies Road complex. John, who has been with Sinclairs for some nine years, carries a clear 10 tonnes on his 17-tonne GVW four-wheeler, the load hidden beneath the sheets in this case being bleach destined for South Wales.

longest of the six used, so that roadside repairs could be carried out in minutes. The Ford Trader was never going to be an AEC, but it did give value for money. Sinclairs costed it that they could fit a new Ford replacement engine during one day at half the price it would cost to overhaul a Mercury engine which took a week of the fitter's time. Looked at that way, the Ford D-series became very acceptable for four-wheeler work and at one time about 20 of these were in use.

At the heavier end, Sinclairs stayed faithful to the Mandator right to the end. To decide upon subsequent replacements during 1975, they ran the ERF B-series in comparative trials with a Volvo F88-290. The Volvo was to win that battle and first the 88s and then the F10s were used as heavyweight traction until the mid-1980s.

As a base of operations, Sinclair had moved into premises on Worcester Road Industrial Estate which had originally been a depot for Bulmers Cider. Strangely, the relaxation of goods vehicle speed limits had meant the Evesham depot was superfluous to Bulmers. Before Sinclairs could make full use of the place, they had to knock down the 4ft-high loading deck which had been needed for the brewers' fleet.

1975 was to see the Sinclair fleet peak around the 40 mark after they had bought the interests of Alan Brown Transport Ltd and Jackson Haulier Bidford Ltd, both of which had previously also worked out of Worcester Road. The final move to their current base at Davies Road was done in October 1983 when the interests of Deryck A. Hartwell were taken over, although the Worcester Road base was kept in use until 1987.

The Sinclair adoption of the DAF marque resulted from Ron's search for a full sleeper-cab fitment on a rigid four-wheeler to upgrade his Ford D-series units. With this spec becoming available on the DAF 2100, about 10 of these vehicles were taken into Sinclair service. They did the job so well that Sinclair then decided to replace the F10s with DAF 3300 4x2 tractors to take them into the heaviest 38-tonne market. Unlike some hauliers, Sinclairs have tended to stay faithful to one particular marque at a time. They reckon it is far easier to learn everything there is to know about one single make and so be able to standardize on all the relevant bits and pieces. Whilst the AECs certainly did them proud, it was first Volvo and now DAF who have continued to carry the Sinclair name. A lot has changed since Ron Sinclair first loaded up his old ambulance with two tons of vegetables, yet in essence the DAF 95-350 simply continues a reliable service that has gone on unbroken for over 40 years.

Fleet list

R. Sinclair Ltd

DAF 1900 4x2 rigid platforms

E619 JNP
E620 JNP
E742 LWP

DAF 95-350 4x2 artic tractor units

E621 JNP	F714 SUY
E622 JNP	F646 TAB
E623 JNP	F858 WNP
E743 LWP	F859 WNP
E744 LWP	F860 WNP
F444 RAB	F861 WNP
F581 RNP	F862 WNP
F582 RNP	G832 KNP
F241 SAB	G833 KNP

DAF 3300 4x2 artic tractor units

B281 EAB
B519 HUY
B529 KNP*
(*owned by Mac Taylor but run on subcontract in Sinclair colours)

The DAF 95-350 is now firmly established as the Sinclair flagship, and customers requirements necessitate more and more the use of curtainsider semi-trailers. Terry Sinclair is seen here loading Ian Gittuf's outfit in February 1991, the Clark 3-ton fork-lift handling a pallet of beans for delivery to Downton near Salisbury. Driver Gittuf joined Sinclairs straight from school as a 16-year-old, progressing from the garage to a four-wheeler and eventually an artic; good service has won him the chance to be entrusted with one of Sinclairs finest.

4: Chris Miller Ltd

It's a fact of transport life that very few family concerns last much more than two or three generations. The complexities of family trees plus periods like recession and rationalization have all combined to make continuity at best awkward and at worst just impossible. Success doesn't necessarily help, either: there are regularly situations where a highly successful business makes itself a prime candidate to be sold out. So finding that Preston-based Chris Miller Ltd can trace their transport life back to 1837 makes them fairly unique. The first Chris Miller set up as a carter in the town at that time and, five generations later, another Chris Miller, together with his cousin John Miller, are still very active, in a business of very diverse nature. With about 50 employees on the current payroll, the company emphasis has swung away from reliance on general haulage. It's now cranage, fork-lifts, industrial and machinery installations, and warehousing, as well as moving the occasional 100-ton load, which keeps the Miller team busy. If that isn't a wide enough range of tasks, then there's aluminium forming and fabrication, with roofing sheets of up to 140ft in length made and of course delivered by Millers to anywhere in the UK from their Preston HQ.

This latter facet of Millers' work has only become prevalent in the last six or seven years, but it underlines a continuing Miller formula. Grandfather Chris Miller was quoted as saying in 1929 that he had never refused to do a transport job on account of its magnitude. Weights of up to 15 tons had already been moved by then, the biggest vehicle he'd had in use being a 6-ton Leyland. For it is a Miller knack of being able to turn their hand to alternatives that has continually stood them in good stead as the fortunes of others have ebbed and flowed.

The first Chris Miller would have had little thought of his later diversity in 1837, for all he knew was that he and his wife Sarah had to do something to improve their lot. Living at Nether Kellet near Carnforth, they decided to move the 25 miles south to the brighter lights of Preston. With one horse and one cart, they offered the services of carting, maximum load being 2 tons. The Millers first set up home at 13 Markland Street but a 200-yard move across to Mona Place, off Croft Street, found them ideally situated. The new house was at the centre of industrialized operations, with a brewery, builder and cotton mill adjacent to them and all obviously in need of a willing carter. The location proved so good that Millers are still in the same place 150 years later.

Chris's son Henry Miller followed him into the business in due course and the nearby forests began to source some traffic, with timber being hauled to the local sawmills. But Preston was still the hub of Millers' work. The rates fixed at a meeting of the Master Carters of the town in the Port Admiral Inn on Lancaster Road in March 1875 make interesting reading. The standard payment for a complete day's hire of a single cart was fixed at 9/– (45p); strangely, if you wanted to hire a cart to work on a Saturday then the rate was reduced to 8/–. No tariff was given on the schedule for Sunday work, implying that, 115 years ago, the Sabbath was unquestionably a day of rest.

Henry Miller's son, born in 1869, was named Chris after his grandfather. He too entered the carting business but his greatest love was the shipping that worked out of Morecambe Bay into the Irish Sea. He intently studied the rigging of the ships and saw how, by using a system of pulleys or blocks, a small amount of effort could be multiplied to perform the hardest of tasks. As Chris took over the business from his father he developed this expertise in power multiplication by taking the techniques into the woods and demonstrating how, rightly used, it meant that the heaviest of trees could be lifted on to reinforced carts and moved in one piece. Such a service was a boon to the timber industry and also saved a huge amount of time and effort that had been expended in chopping huge

CK 406 was new to Millers in 1921 and, like all the first nine Leylands which they bought, it was taxed to haul a drawbar trailer. These egg boxes are being unloaded near Preston Public Hall: note how clever use has been made of the raves along the body edge to tip the load in towards the centre of the vehicle. This four-wheeler was known as an RAF type because Leyland built over 5,000 of them for the Royal Flying Corps (predecessor to the RAF). Many were bought back from the government by the manufacturer for reconditioning and subsequent resale.

trees into smaller, manageable lengths.

Only the strongest of horses could be used for this heavyweight hauling, three of the special shires of that time being known as Dally, Duke and Bonney. Getting the best out of them was down to men like Joseph Hampton and Jack Tickle for, unlike the modern-day truck, you couldn't just walk away from the horses on a night without seeing to their needs, especially if they were a bit off colour. Joe Hampton recalled that if any of the horses were ill then he would mix a concoction of linseed and treacle in boiling water which he would cart by the bucket-load from his house in Talbot Street to the stables in Croft Street. He'd even spend the night with them to make sure they were alright, such was the relationship that men and horses shared.

In 1892, Preston Dock was opened and a whole new range of goods were expected to be moved by Millers' carts. They still specialized in timber, with huge specimens hauled all of 40 miles to Garston at Liverpool. Real long-distance stuff, this, in the horse-power era but most of the men managed to get back to Preston for a Friday night, as this was pay night. The ritual reportedly saw the men queue outside the front window of the Mona Place house as the money was handed through. The twist to this weekly performance was that, if Miller felt you hadn't worked hard enough, he wasn't averse to taking something out of your pay-packet.

In 1920 Millers' fleet was reckoned as 10 strong, all horse and cart teams, but in 1921 Chris was to enter the motorized age, buying CK 406, the first of many brand-new Leylands. Only rated as a four-tonner, the petrol-engined four-wheeler was taxed to haul a drawbar trailer and of course all sorts of tasks were expected of it. Long-length timber naturally filled its back but a more strange wooden object in the guise of a 40ft-long, 16ft-wide, 14ft-high office building was an early job, being moved in one piece from one side of Preston docks to the other. Picking it up and of course putting it back down without cracking even a pane

Moving hen houses was another aspect of the poultry trade for Millers. One load of incubators which they moved and stored for the Royal Lancashire Show on behalf of a Dutch manufacturer caused them trouble when there was an argument over the rate charged and Millers had to argue their case at Preston County Court. Judge Oliver awarded them £15 14s and costs.

In 1932, when horses were still widely in use, the Miller fleet of Leylands formed an impressive display. Although there have been modifications and extensions to the premises, Millers have occupied the same site, bordering Mona Place, Croft Street and Lodge Street, for their entire history. Chris Miller is third from the left of the group in the centre of this photo, whilst Jack Miller, left, and Arthur Miller, fourth from left, sport trilby hats, deemed to be quite racy in this bowler-hatted era.

of glass was achieved using that same Miller knack which had moved trees longer than 100ft with impunity. Millers had long established a reputation for moving and installing things like gas tanks, the bonus of the motorized Leylands being that loads could be moved much quicker, and it obviously made long distances easier.

Chris took his two sons Arthur and Jack into the business more or less straight from school. Jack served his time at Leyland Motors and then worked as a mate on the new-fangled petrol lorry to learn his craft that way. 'Arty' was expected to concentrate on the administrative side of things,

being qualified as an accountant. Both were to learn something during the depression of 1926, for when everyone around them was trying to sell whatever they had, Chris took the opportunity of buying land round the Mona Place depot and invested in a huge warehouse further up Croft Street, adjacent to his own land. Whilst the wagons stood about doing nothing, Millers' men were busy building a new high-lofted garage. Incorporating a lifting beam that could support 10 tons and doors that opened to 70ft wide, the design was way ahead of what was needed and is still more than useful 65 years later.

In 1930 the brass plate of Chris Miller Ltd was affixed to the Mona Place door but Chris didn't have long to admire it, for on October 29, 1933, his sudden death meant Jack and Arthur were left in control. But the seeds had already been sown as both sons inherited the theory and joy of putting into practice the Miller knack of doing things their own way.

Whilst horses were still being used up to 1935, the brothers continued to invest in Leylands. Their first Buffalo is particularly remembered as being able to live up to its name. It soon became apparent that the men who worked this heavyweight four-wheeler always looked as though they had just been in a fight. Black eyes, cuts and grazes about the face, broken teeth or even a broken arm were quite regular occurrences, and if they were asked how they had come by their injuries they would always blame Jack. No,

they didn't mean the boss, Jack Miller: 'Jack' was short for jack handle, which in turn was a variant of starting handle. When the truth really came out, it was the kick-back on the handle of the Buffalo which caused so much pain. That was the sole reason electric starters were specified – before Millers ran out of drivers!

During the Second World War, a wide range of traffic was moved but then in the late 1940s it was textiles that became more important. Working in a triangular sort of pattern, the Miller fleet would first move the raw bales of cotton from the docks at Liverpool out to the mills in Oldham, Shaw and Rochdale. Spun into yarn, it would then be loaded for north Lancashire to be processed into finished cloth which in turn would be hauled back to Liverpool for export to the world.

In 1949, the nationalization programme rippled round

36

Opposite: If you go to White Cross Bay on Lake Windermere now you will find a caravan site but in the 1940s the area was used by Short Bros to build Sunderland flying boats. About 1950, the huge hangars were stripped down and Millers moved this 90ft section from the lake side to Liverpool. The crew, here stopped en route near Preston, were Jack Ashton, centre, and Jimmy Murphy, on the right. Bob Baron, on the left, has now retired but is still a regular visitor to the Miller yard on Fridays.

Opposite, below: Millers used ex-RAF trailers as bogies for long loads, but they also invested in a purpose-built outfit for their early forays into heavy haulage. The Scammell, here with Jimmy Murphy behind the wheel, was bought from Shell Chemicals and is coupled to a Dyson semi-trailer. The low-loader had a knock-out back end which allowed this 18-ton trenching machine to self load. Eaves were a large building contractor and Millers moved their RB cranes as well, until the Blackpool-based concern went bust.

Crane number 8 was this eight-wheeler, the Thornycroft Trusty chassis having been bought second-hand from Shell. The crane was a Coles 1210S, and Millers were charged £5,925 in June 1958 for the machine to be mounted on the wagon. An extra £60 covered the fitting of dynamic braking to the crane's lowering motion. Bob Whiteside is the crane driver here, busy erecting a three-piece glazed canopy section to cover a walkway between two neighbouring premises of the Preston grocery firm E. H. Booth.

the country and Millers were to lose two of their long-distance 'A'-licensed vehicles. The two brothers sensed this was a time to act again, whilst most in haulage were in a total state of depression. Apparently their father Chris had a habit of saying, 'When one door closes, another one opens.' But he then followed this up by adding, 'But you've got to be bloody quick to get your foot in fast before it shuts again!'

Looking at what hadn't been nationalized, Millers decided to go first into removals and in 1950 they took over Kirkham Removals Ltd. This was run as a separate entity by the brothers' sister Jenny Lambert until Jenny retired about 1960 and Kirkhams was sold again as a going concern to Brewer & Turnbull Ltd. Another area exempt from

nationalization was heavy haulage, and the brothers were to buy their first, second-hand Scammell from one of the petrol companies. They also went into mobile cranage, which of course didn't require licences at all as cranes weren't deemed to be goods vehicles.

Their first mobile lifter, the Taylor Hydracrane, wasn't anything very grand but it was still fairly unusual. The story about Taylors of Salford is also quite interesting: they had fallen upon their design idea after they had been obliged to use a tipper vehicle to lift something in the factory. With a rope slung over the body and kept taut, the effect of raising the tipper was to lift what was tied on to the end of the rope. This basic concept triggered off their first offerings, with a fixed-length jib lifted by a pair of

HCK 321 was Millers' first brand-new heavy-haulage Scammell. It came into service in 1954 as a 25-ton ballast-box tractor but was soon converted to artic tractor form. In this 1963 picture, it has a temporary ballast box on its back and Bill Ellis at the wheel. He and Maurice Swords in the following Comet are about to leave Blackpool with these fairly light pressure vessels. The leading trailer sports Miller-made fabric mudguards at the rear, whilst the Leyland is coupled to a BTC semi-trailer of 10-ton capacity.

Taylor Hydra were taken over by Coles Cranes, though the name was kept for the continuing old-type models. 'Speed Crane' is a bit of a misnomer because this little 4-tonner was anything but fast. A similar 10-ton version is made, the main difference being its use of outriggers. Tommy Southworth is the crane driver here, whilst the rigger on the load of lathes is Jos Robinson. Dick Harrison is the driver of the well liked AEC Mercury: he now drives cranes for Millers.

tipper-pattern rams. Millers bought their Taylor crane No 1 in 1950 at an ex-RAF surplus sale along with some long, low-slung trailers as well as a distinctive David Brown winching tractor that had been used originally for towing aircraft about. The miscellany of bits and pieces bought in these sales rekindled the Miller knack of moving all sorts of improbable loads. Massive 90ft girders were moved from Windermere to Liverpool and similar oversize sections of Mulberry Harbour were hauled with impunity from the south coast up to Preston docks. But whilst these jobs caught the headlines, it was behind-the-scenes lifting and shifting that really earned Millers their keep as removals of an industrial type proved to be their special art.

Weaving looms were one load in particular where Millers shone, as these things were particularly difficult both to move and then to load up on to a vehicle. The Miller system had the loom jacked just far enough from the ground to allow a set of skates to be inserted underneath, then it could be dragged out of the shop. Out in the open

air, the Taylor Hydracrane made easy work of the lift, so that a loom could often be dispatched on its way in minutes rather than the hours previously needed for loading.

These assorted techniques allowed Millers to continue to expand their operations. A change in the family involvement occurred when the fifth generation began to take over the reins in the late 1960s, although Arthur Miller was to live until 1977, elder brother Jack having died in December 1973. Being the third Chris Miller to take the helm didn't daunt the youngster and over the last 25 years he and cousin John have been involved in some of the strangest of jobs.

In 1972, they were doing a small amount of work at the new Seaforth Container terminal which was under construction at the mouth of the River Mersey. They saw that huge boulders were being brought on to the construction site, some weighing in at 10 tons a piece which meant there were only two rocks on the back of a 32-tonner. The most noticeable thing about the job was how the his shot, taken about 1967, epitomizes the industrial side of Millers' work. Loaded up om the tackle store, these vehicles would arry skates, jacks, chain blocks, turfors nd all the other assorted gear which, when xpertly used, could move and install lmost anything. Millers have had good ervice from the Hyster fork-lifts like the ne suspended here: they have three of nese 10,000lb versions and the first, ought in 1964, is still in use.

lillers were involved in some of the ardest work in their history during the onstruction of the Seaforth terminal. hunting this road-going trailer is one of vo Leyland Beavers they used on the site. hey had originally started out as platform ur-wheelers hauling drawbar trailers and ere then converted into artic units and sed on Joshua Tetley brewery work. A urther 12 months of far harder work at eaforth followed after they had come to ne end of their useful life on the road.

hauliers involved kept changing. When they enquired about that, the reason given was that no one could keep up with the work. It wasn't the run across from the North Wales quarries that created problems, it was the demanding two-mile haul on site to where the huge rocks were being unloaded to form the primary armour of the sea wall. Millers were asked if they wanted a go at the work, they agreed to a single week's trial, the Croft Street thinking caps were put on and a better solution devised.

Instead of using road wagons to run across site, Millers bought three battered shunters – two old Beavers and an old Bristol – and they picked up the trailers that were left on the site edge. The semi-trailers involved were protected with a carpeting of railway sleepers and worked a three-shift system to cover the 24-hour day, six days a week. The early trial ran on to a continuous year's work which meant, all told, 120,000 tons of rock were moved. The vehicle abuse was still phenomenal but the Atkinson Borderers did Millers proud, though the men spent many nights changing springs in the street or performing other necessary tasks just to keep the wheels turning. There were also casualties among the trailers, like the one that broke in half when a 25-ton boulder was accidentally dropped on its back.

It was back amongst the rocks of North Wales at the end

To supplement the two Beavers at Seaforth, Chris Miller bought this ex-BRS Bristol, an 'old banger', he called it, as another shunter. It is seen moving some 50ft piling bars, among the easier work it was expected to perform. It is also on a better part of the site here: the heavyweight sling was kept permanently through the front towing eyes so that when it regularly got stuck in the morass a passing Euclid could tow it out in moments.

39

of the 1970s that Millers made the headlines, broke records and generally demonstrated that small fish could still swim quite actively in the same sea as bigger fish. Their involvement at Dinorwic has been well chronicled before. Really, it was having the 'nous' to do things more efficiently that won them praise from people who realized what they had achieved. It takes some believing, but what was originally planned as 24 voyages of an expensive ro-ro Fisher boat was trimmed to seven when Millers demonstrated how to make the most of the space and time available. Whilst their newly bought big Mack 'Bonzo Bear' may have made the pictures, Chris Miller will probably tell you that it was their tubs and girders which should really receive the accolades.

Moving all the water-handling equipment for Dinorwic, plus all the spin-off work involved, cushioned Millers to the recessional effects of the early 1980s but they didn't pass the company by completely. A big casualty were some contract vehicles on local distribution, with work for ten of them lost when Joshua Tetley brewery traffic disappeared after their new owner Ind Coope reorganized their own depots.

Other work sourced from Millers' 40,000 square feet of warehousing dried up too, but as that door closed another door in the shape of a telephone enquiry was soon to open. That first contact with what is now Hoogovens Aluminium developed to change completely the working pattern of the

Miller team. In 1983 it may have been difficult for anyone in Croft Street to imagine a 100ft-long roofing strip but now the company are producing, palletizing, loading and delivering strips close to 140ft long – but that's only when they keep the garage doors open and load straight out on to the road. Millers have even turned their hand to engineering aluminium in their own right: just like making a set of special bogies out of a Volvo F86 chassis to move railway carriages, it is really straightforward stuff if you've got the knack.

In 1987, Millers celebrated their 150th anniversary, in a fairly quiet fashion, of course. When questioned about the Miller formula for staying in business, Chris was quoted as saying, 'We think there is a place for the small, resourceful and reliable company that provides a personal service and continuity. We have stayed small and are still here while others have gone screaming past us only to fall over themselves. But while we have no intention of going backwards, we have no plans to start acquiring a lot of other businesses or to be part of anyone else's empire. We are intent on carrying on as a family concern.' And his closing remark, 'We now intend to expand in areas not wholly in our traditional business,' would, I'm sure, have had those first four generations of Millers on their feet to applaud the continued use of the family's inventive flair and imagination.

'Bonzo Bear' was a star of the 1978 Birmingham Motor Show. Although the vehicle hasn't been perfect, it has done some phenomenal work and is one of the main reasons why Millers are so well known. Peter Beasley is seen at the wheel of the Mack in 1979 with its original narrow rear bogie. The load is an 80-ton engine set, supported on five rows of Commetto, which Millers removed from a factory at Ambergate, Derbyshire. It was to be transhipped onto a Planthaul outfit for subsequent delivery on the Continent.

Fleet list

Chris Miller Ltd

Reg no	Make/type
LWR 101P	Seddon Atkinson artic 'Lift 'n Shift'
GCW 520S	Ford 'D' 4x2 rigid
VCT 140S	Seddon Atkinson artic unit
NFV 803T	Mack 6x4 ballast box/artic tractor 'Bonzo Bear'
DDA 23V	Ford 'D' 4x2 7.5t van
JLK 255V	Ford 'D' 4x2 rigid flat
LLE 587V	Volvo F12 6x4 artic unit
THG 403V	Seddon Atkinson artic unit
UBV 392V	Seddon Atkinson artic unit
WHG 563V	Thornycroft Antar 6x4 ballast box tractor
EMB 308X	Seddon Atkinson artic unit
WUM 930X	Seddon Atkinson artic unit
B954 REA	Leyland Freighter 4x2 flat Hiab
B516 UNG	Seddon Atkinson 301 artic unit
D325 CTR	Mercedes-Benz 609D 4x2 rigid
D225 MNA	Volvo FL6 4x2 flat Hiab
D678 PKK	Ford Transit fitters' van

Cranes

Fleet no	Reg no	Capacity (tons)	Make/type
26	ACW 448R	15	Hydracon Clansman truck-mounted
28	OFV 396T	8	Hydracon Marksman truck-mounted
31	YBV 105V	15	PH S15 all-terrain
32	RVT 907R	10	Coles Speedcrane low-headroom
33	RDE 451S	25	Grove TMS 250 truck-mounted
35	A736 RWS	18	Coles 18/22 truck-mounted
36	F545 YCW	35	Faun RTF33 all-terrain
37	JRN 472S	45	Coles 45/50 truck-mounted

Fork-lift trucks

Fleet no	Reg no	Capacity (lb)	Make/type
4	ACK 134B	10,000	Hyster S100B
7	ECK 998E	10,000	Hyster S100B
8	HCK 657G	4,000	Hyster S40
11	KCK 418H	4,000	Hyster S40
12	PCK 807K	5,000	Hyster S50
16	VTB 282L	4,000	Hyster S40
20	RHG 818X	15,000	Hyster S150B
21	EBV 681W	10,000	Hyster S100
22	unreg'd	8,000	Hyster S80B

5: Sayers Transport Services (Newbury) Ltd

If ever anyone in the road haulage industry wanted to illustrate the best possible image of a transport machine, they would be hard put to it to find a better example than one of the current flagships in the Sayers Transport Services fleet. Sayers operate premium Scanias in two-tone blue livery and, whilst company headquarters is a custom-built base on the outskirts of Thatcham in Berkshire, you may quite well spot 'Wessex Musketeer' or 'Wessex Gladiator' in the heart of Denmark or even in southern France. Providing a service for the bulk haulage of polymers and powders has taken the company anywhere and everywhere in Europe. But, like many firms in the transport business, it had humble beginnings.

It was grandfather Wilfred Sayers who was responsible for embarking the family on a transport life. His home was the small village of Brightwalton, midway between Newbury and Wantage, and the only reliable way for residents to get either themselves or their goods to and from the markets in the early 1900s was to use the horse and cart of Wilf Sayers. He had no great aspirations for dramatic expansion, but the arrival of the mechanized age saw him adopt the trading name of W.J. Sayers & Sons, an impressive enough title for his single, dark blue vehicle. Sacks of coal, hauled the eight miles from Newbury and sold on to the households of the village, were what kept his business going.

Round about 1945, it was the 'Sons' in the name, Arthur and Philip, who came back from the war and into the firm and decided to build up the service that Sayers offered. For tools they took to Albion four-wheelers and, befitting their rural location, they relied mainly on agricultural sources of traffic, taking on the cutting and stripping of timber as well as transporting it. Whilst the period of nationalization turned much of the industry on its head, the shock waves passed the localized operations of the Sayers without effect. Come 1953, which brought a surge of ex-BRS vehicles on to the market, the brothers took the opportunity of picking up a few 'A'-licensed vehicles to go with their contract 'C', 'B' and 'B' licences with extensions. The mish-mash of licensing reflects the wide variety of activity for the Sayers fleet which was to reach double figures about 1957, a sign that they should be incorporated, their adopted name being the current one, Sayers Transport Services (Newbury) Ltd.

Base was still at Brightwalton, with the day-to-day roles of the two brothers seeing Arthur in charge of traffic, paperwork and administration whilst all aspects of the mechanical side of the business came to brother Phil. Keeping the maturing fleet on the road was made marginally easier in 1956 for that year heralded the first brand-new vehicle to come into service, painted in the newly adopted livery of two-tone blue. That sole Albion Chieftain, MRX 202, may not have been particularly outstanding but to 11-year-old Philip 'Pip' Sayers, son of Arthur and current Managing Director, it was to be his passport to the outside world beyond Brightwalton as he accompanied regular driver 'Walt' on his journeys to all parts of the country.

With the fleet of Albions operated from the side of the Sayers' thatched cottage home, the smell of diesel soon had far more influence on the growing Pip than any schooling he received. He had to wait until the age of 16 before he could officially start work for the company and till 17 before his car licence would allow him to drive a rather old but fairly light little Albion. Its official unladen weight of '2ton 19cwt 3qrs' just scraped under the three-ton borderline for HGVs but the flat was also asked to support a payload that regularly ran to nine tons. Close to 10 years old when he got it, that Albion put Pip through the mangle as it taught him a lot about driving and a lot about life. With nothing in the way of pulling power from its tired engine or stopping power from its worn brakes, it was a matter of praying whether you would get over the tops of some of the

This Chieftain four-wheeler, MRX 202, was the first Albion Sayers bought brand-new, going into service in 1956. Pictured on the back lawn of the Sayers' Brightwalton depot and home, it had a long-wheelbase chassis and four-cylinder engine. The platform body was built by Sayers themselves, and they also fitted a long-range fuel tank so that regular trips to Liverpool and Sheffield could be undertaken without refuelling. Walter Bailey was the regular driver of this Albion. Below right: photographed at Brightwalton in about 1968 are two of the three AEC Marshal six-wheeled flats with Park Royal cabs that Sayers ran. Pip Sayers remembers fleet number 20 well because it was the first brand-new vehicle he was entrusted with. Fitted with a light-alloy body made by Musselwhite of Romsey and capable of carrying 16 tons of payload, the AEC had the AV470 engine and twin fuel tanks totalling 60 gallons. Of equal note in this CVRTC photograph is the demountable grain tipping body, made by Tamplin, on the Marshal at the back. Getting it on and off the platform was done by sheer brute strength.

fearsome climbs that the local Downs threw up in front of you, then praying even more that you could stop on the way down the other side. With agriculture still a big part of Sayers' traffic, catching sacks of barley straight off the farm conveyor belt at two hundredweight a time was how Pip, like many other drivers of the past, contracted back problems that were to stay with him for the rest of his life.

New Albion Chieftains and Reivers started to arrive but, after a phase of mechanical problems with them, the company decided to change marques about 1962. That year saw the arrival of the first AEC Mercury and, befitting its name, the model is remembered for being extremely fleet of foot. Having the older Park Royal cab, with entry gained by climbing in over the front wheel, it was still a driver's favourite because of its rapid pace of knots. Though it was only a four-wheeler rated to 14 tons gross, a 10-ton payload was well within the ability of its AV470 engine. The same engine powered the lightweight six-wheeled Marshal, and Sayers were one of the first in the area to run the 22-ton GVW six-leggers when the weight legislation was uprated in 1965.

The new law then allowed four-wheelers to run at 16 tons GVW but for the old 14-ton Mercury some mods were needed to take advantage of this extra capacity. Sayers were running a few of these four-wheelers and one of them had a narrowed inboard front axle and had to stay at 14 tons. The others were equipped with power-assisted handbrakes and allowed to run at 15 tons GVW, the step up to 16 tons only being permitted if complicated power-assisted steering was also plumbed into the chassis.

During the 1960s, the family influence at Sayers strengthened. Pip's brother Stuart, always known as Gabby, came to work in the extended Nissen hut garage in 1964. Four years later Philip senior's son Malcolm, today's fleet engineer, who had completed a full mechanic's apprenticeship, also joined the family firm. Malcolm's brother John Sayers, who now runs the traffic office, came into the fold in 1972 but by then the whole look and direction of Sayers had begun to change.

During the 1960s, the Sayers fleet had stabilized around the 12 to 15 mark, a mixture of flats and tippers run on a

mixture of licences. The change to the 'O' category operators' licensing in '68 lifted many constraints including an inbuilt declaration of the licensed vehicle's unladen weight. Sayers took advantage of this new relaxation by going into articulation. The Mercury in tractor-unit form ran up to 26 tons gross and the heavyweight AEC Mandators were bought for work at the highest, 32-ton mark. The new artic concept should have worked well with the company's favoured marque of AEC but in truth it didn't. There were six or eight Mandators run, all sporting the Ergomatic style of cab that other Leyland Group vehicles of the time were using and Sayers were eventually to suffer problems similar to those experienced by other Leyland vehicle users in that era. Difficulties right across the board were recalled, engine breakdowns, gearboxes falling to pieces and even trouble encountered with the propshafts.

With a relatively small fleet, these mechanical problems became hard for Arthur and Phil Sayers to bear. What made it worse was that they had won some new work for a company that had just set up in business at Thatcham. This concern was involved with the production of polymers, an important aspect of the fast-growing plastics industry, and the prospect of even more work was there but could only be contemplated if a reliable delivery pattern was guaranteed. Unfortunately the AECs weren't giving this, and one day, with three Mandators lying crippled in the yard, sheer frustration drove Arthur to pick up the telephone. He put a call in to the local Scania dealer who had been pestering him. 'Bring one up and let's have a look at it,' was all that was said, but Arthur spent all afternoon walking between his office and the yard, inspecting that Swedish machine.

At the time, the Scania was a relatively unknown quantity in the UK and it certainly wasn't being offered for sale on the basis of being cheap. Prices at the time are remembered as putting the AEC Mandator around the £3,000 mark whilst the Scania 110 4x2 tractor unit was about 50% more expensive at about £4,500. The two brothers thought long and hard about what to do: call it intuition, good judgement or just plain good luck, the decision was made to invest £9,000 in buying BJB 990J and BRX 13J, the first two 110s to come into Sayers' fleet. These new Scanias were also to herald an entirely new type of service, as consultation with the customer led to the carriage of polymer in bulk in a 1,450cu ft Crane Fruehauf pressure-discharge belly tanker. If this didn't strike anyone as a new departure it certainly made an impression to learn that the new Sayers' outfit was running to the mainland of Europe to pick up loads for import back into the UK. True, the traffic was collected only 5 kilometres down the road from the landing port at Le Havre, but it was the start of a Continental service that Sayers were to excel at.

Repeat orders for more Scanias continued until 1974. Then, trying to buy three new tractors very quickly, Sayers were thwarted by being quoted excessively long delivery times as the Scania's popularity soared. It was MAN, just

coming into the UK, who got the order instead, thr[ee] 16.232s being supplied almost immediately at a ve[ry] attractive price. These three vehicles were all fitted with th[e] ZF 12-speed gearbox operated by a column-mount[ed] gearlever which was recalled as being rather strange at fir[st] although most drivers managed once they had got used [to] them. The trio did quite well but they were rather heavy o[n] fuel and had difficulties with their splitter boxes, so n[o] further MANs made inroads into Sayers' Scania preferenc[e.]

When Sayers first discovered the joys o[f] articulation, they adopted the AEC Mandator as their preferred traction. UB[L] 895G was their first big AEC and its firs[t] driver was Cyril Mason who, after 34 years[] service, is still at Sayers as warehous[e] manager. The AEC is coupled to a Tasker[s] tipping trailer, the body it carries having been built by Tamplin of Chicheste[r] specifically for grain traffic.

Unreliability proved to be a problem with the AEC artic unit and Sayers changed over to Scania, a marque which is still in favour with them. Although they have tended to standardize on the 110–113 range, 'Wessex Ranger' was one of two rather heavy and expensive 140s they ran. The name 'Spindle' signwritten just below the headboard indicates that the vehicle's regular driver was Simon Sayers. Here seen westbound on the A12 in Essex, the Scania artic tipper tended to run an unusual mixture of grain out to the Midlands and coal back-loaded for the south.

Above left: 'Wessex Chieftain' was one of a pair of Scania 81s, companion to 'Wessex Knight', registered YJM 124T (though the 'Chieftain' name had first been used on NBL 332L, a 4x2 Scania 80). Sayers opted for the lighter weight 81s and Volvo F7s to maximize payloads within the 32 tons gross limit. Photographed at Newbury in August 1982 by John Henderson, 'Chieftain' had Alan Gibson as regular driver. The semi-trailer is a 1,600cu ft Carmichael which is still in use although it has since been converted to tri-axle form. All that remains of the cannibalized 'Chieftain' at Newbury today is a pair of chassis rails. Above right: Sayers' preference for Scania extended to rigids too: 'Wessex Monarch' was one of two model 81 four-wheelers that the haulier used for 10-ton loads of palletized goods. As the Stalybridge location of this event suggests, this vehicle, HJH 153W, tended to work the Manchester and North-West area. The name 'Monarch' had first been used on a Scania 111, fleet number 46, registered KDP 485P. Below: the Sayers fleet lined up at Thatcham in 1983 makes an impressive sight. Outnumbered by all those Scanias is the sole DAF 3300 the company ever ran. 'Wessex Brigadier' was offered to Sayers by Chipping Motors at High Wycombe as a long-term demonstrator and was bought after the trial period, although regular driver Mick James always found the DAF's fuel consumption rather heavy when compared with the 112s. It was sold after a few years' service.

'Wessex Gladiator' is seen resting not f
from the home of its regular driver, Joh
Nendick, at Charltons on the edge of th
North York Moors. Since this shot wa
taken in June 1988, John has moved clos
to his base at Gainsborough and he is als
now the proud driver of a new Scania 11
A942 AMO is still in service but Sayer
tend to use it just as a spare tractor a
Thatcham and at the time of writing it
next in line for replacement.

1974 also saw an arrival of an entirely different kind when owner-driver Roy Davies came knocking on the door and asked if he could provide additional traction for Sayers with his Volvo F86 unit. 16 years on, Roy is still hauling semi-trailers for the company, and he has now progressed to a Scania 143 as his current tractor unit. Roy was to be the first of nine other owner-drivers who were to work exclusively for Sayers although not all run in the fleet colours and not all are using Scanias.

As the 110s and 111s led to 112s, the only complaint against these big Swedes was that an ever-increasing girth cut into their payload. Coupled to a tanker, they could only squeeze on about 19 tons when running at the 32-ton limit. Specifically to counter that difficulty, a quartet of Volvo F7s were bought: running with tanks, they could carry another ton and a half of fee-earning cargo within that same 32-ton limit.

The trend towards almost total articulation, with full-length flat and tank trailers, meant the fleet's home base at Brightwalton was close to bursting point. 1978 was to see Sayers move to a green-field site off Colthrop Lane in Thatcham to set up their current base. Running the fleet, 'Pip' Sayers took over command as his father and uncle stepped down to take things more easily. The Sayers'

Arguably the best-known vehicle in the Sayers fleet is this AEC 6x6 which is the pride and joy of Stuart 'Gabby' Sayers. Although very much at home on the vintage or concours rally field, 'Tiny' is also a working truck, with snow ploughing and recovery as just two of its regular tasks. Here, it demonstrates another of its roles, transhipping or unloading big bags of granules for onward delivery in bulk. This vehicle, like most in the Sayers fleet, shows off the fine talents of signwriter Tim Boyle.

With the modern generation of tipping tankers being built to the maximum dimensions legally allowed, a lot of thought has been given to stability, especially when in the tipping mode. The latest truck to be called 'Wessex Chieftain', regular driver Kevin Hill, demonstrates how the LAG tipping ram is mounted directly above the fifth-wheel coupling. Sayers also dump the air from the semi-trailer suspension units when tipping and use wind-down landing legs to provide a stable tripod effect.

administration was set to move further afield with the setting up of an office at Stalybridge to organize traffic in and out of the North-West, but it was a development in Lincolnshire that was to have the biggest long-term effect on the company.

The new depot which opened at Gainsborough in December 1984, like the office at Stalybridge, was a response to the changing pattern of customer demands. But unlike the one on the other side of the Pennines, the 10-acre site in Lincolnshire was the premises of a joint venture under the name of S de R (Transport & Warehousing) Ltd. As its name suggests, 50% of the involvement was Sayers, the other partner being De Rijke, a large haulier based at Spijkenisse near Rotterdam with a 450-strong fleet running throughout Europe. The new arrangement at Gainsborough meant continuing bulk operations in a big way, so it's understandable that Sayers leapt at the new 38 tonnes legislation, announced in May 1983, to broaden their payload capacity. Following the Continental influence, the company chose and has stayed with the 2+3 axle configuration. The little Volvo F7 was tried up to 36 tonnes, but at the heaviest weight band the Scania was to come into its own and currently the 113 coupled to a LAG tank running on SAF air suspension is the Sayers' favoured outfit. The present fleet breaks down into a mix of about 60% pressure/tipping tanks with the balance of 40% on general haulage.

Scania might dominate the fleet list but arguably the biggest, most famous, most adaptable and favourite machine – as far as Gabby Sayers is concerned at least – is still an AEC. As far back as anyone can remember, one line of work that Sayers were very active in yet rarely advertised was snow ploughing for the local council. They first started this by putting a blade on one of the old Albion four-wheelers but as these motors became too busy, the company bought

OTO 376, a 4x4 AEC Matador which proved to be a godsend on the tops of the Berkshire Downs. 'Big Daddy', another Matador, ARX 361J, was to take its place, whilst 'Tiny', bought a couple of years ago to supplement it, performs a wide variety of tasks other than just ploughing. The 6x6 AEC crane, wrecker, snow plough and rally exhibit has the official fleet title of 'Wessex Retriever'. It was Gabby Sayers who thought up this naming idea to personalize the vehicles after he had started driving in 1964. The word Wessex derives from the old name for the area round nearby Wantage which was the birthplace of the famous cake-burning King Arthur. The naming has now become very much a part of the Sayers livery, and mention must be made of the expertise of signwriter Tim Boyle. Now in his 70s, Tim has used his freelance talents with Sayers since meeting up with Arthur Sayers when they fought together during the last war. Tim has seen many changes in the profile of the Sayers fleet but perhaps it was during 1990 that the most changes seemed to occur.

In January of that year the numbers increased by six when a previously contracted fleet was absorbed into Sayers as they took over its traffic. Standards weren't allowed to drop, however, and in May 1990, the company achieved the British Standard of Quality Assurance, BS5750. But by then Sayers was in fact in the hands of new owners. The relationship with De Rijke which had first started with that joint venture at Gainsborough in 1984 had grown so strong that on April 11, 1990, the decision was made for the company of Sayers Transport Services to be sold to that large Dutch haulier. On the face of it, though, there has been no apparent change in day-to-day operations. The same Sayers' personnel are still very much involved in the concern, ever aiming to sustain their hard-fought-for reputation which gives such a fine image to the road transport world.

The Sayers livery may not have changed much in close on 40 years but it still has a distinctive and modern look to it. 'Wessex Musketeer' is one of two Sayers outfits on contract to Warwick International. Drivers Terry Hedges and Alan Gibson average about 1,500 miles a week running between North Wales and the Continent carrying powdered commodities. To cut down tyre wear, the semi-trailer bogie can lift two of its three axles when running empty.

Fleet list

Sayers Transport Services

Fleet no	Reg no	Make/model	Axles	Wessex name
67	PJM 344X	Scania 112	4x2	Gunner
69	A942 AMO	Scania 112	4x2	Gladiator
72	B774 EBL	Scania 112	4x2	Cavalier
73	B181 FJH	Scania 112	4x2	Marauder
74	B382 HRD	Scania 112	4x2	Invader
75	B383 HRD	Scania 112	4x2	Bugler
76	C758 MRD	Scania 112	4x2	Grenadier
78	C676 PJH	Scania 112	4x2	Crusader
79	D281 WJB	Scania 112	4x2	Commander
80	D227 ABY	Scania 93	6x2	Guardsman*
81	D226 ABY	Scania 112	4x2	Chieftain
82	D328 DLH	Scania 112	4x2	Ranger
83	E600 JCR	ERF E6	4x2	Monarch*
84	E355 GLK	Scania 112	4x2	Lancer
85	E364 GLK	Scania 112	4x2	Volunteer
86	E199 HLE	Scania 112	4x2	Musketeer
87	F996 OOY	Scania 113	4x2	Brigadier
88	D2 RNE	Scania 112	4x2	
89	F241 JBA	Volvo F10	6x2	
90	F242 JBA	Volvo F10	6x2	
91	G626 PNE	Volvo F10	4x2	
92	G627 PNE	Volvo F10	6x2	
94	G31 XTP	Scania 113	4x2	Buccaneer
95	G32 XTP	Scania 113	4x2	Explorer
96	H953 BTR	Scania 113	4x2	Invincible
97	H952 BTR	Scania 113	4x2	
–	RRX 960H	AEC Militant	6x6	Retriever

*Note: all artic tractor units except nos 80 and 83 (rigids).

5: Watts Bros (Beverley) Ltd

For over 700 years, the skyline round Beverley, always the heartland of the old East Riding of Yorkshire, has been dominated by its inspiring Minster. For more than 112 of those years one of its most famous representatives has been the transport concern of Watts Bros Ltd. Now running a premium fleet close to 50 strong, it offers warehousing and a general haulage service to its customers and has long been a specialist in multi-drop distribution.

Historically, Beverley began very much as a self-contained place, the 500-year-old North Bar being one of the last indicators of the enclosed town's five medieval gates. It prospered through the cloth trade and also, although the North Sea is a 12-mile crow flight away, ship building was a thriving trade: limited space meant boats had to be launched sideways into the River Hull.

In more modern times, however, it was to be the settlement established where the River Hull runs into the Humber – formally called Kingston-upon-Hull, better known to most people simply as Hull – that thrived on the strength of its growing port traffic, and Beverley needed to associate itself with this growing source of prosperity. In 1878, one John Watts began to make his contribution to forging a link between these two Yorkshire towns. Born and bred at Louth in Lincolnshire, Watts bought the carrying business of J. Backhouse Esq, working out of a house and yard in Lairgate, Beverley. It was on the track between there and Hull that, six days a week, every week of the year, the Watts' carts would normally be seen.

The carrier was the life blood of the community in the 19th century. It was he who collected and delivered virtually everything that was moved. Whether it was a hat box from the milliners, a case of wine from the vintners or some select foodstuffs from the grocers, your local carrier would be the one you would get to collect or deliver it. The Watts run started off in Beverley and then went via Woodmansey and Dunswell to terminate in Hull. There were pre-arranged collection points along the way but, because the cart ran more or less like clockwork, if you just waited by the roadside in the early morning you knew it wouldn't be long before Watts appeared. Once at Hull, the deliveries were done and collections made. With these completed, the horse and cart went to Mytongate in the town. Here a series of stands were organized so carriers from all over the region had room to feed the horse and await traders to bring goods to them for delivery on the return journey. Simple but efficient was the carrier system. It depended on men like John Watts who could also be relied on to deliver personal messages on their way. They would even take shoes in for repair – and of course bring them back the same day – and on occasion they would transport farmers' wives up to the big town of Hull for a special day out.

Although the type of traffic on this job was hardly the same two days running, the route that the horse and cart followed was almost identical. The outfit obviously needed a driver, but other vital parts of the Watts service were the lads who assisted him. It was their job to run up and down the alleys of Hull fetching and carrying whilst the driver dealt with the more important tasks. To improve efficiency, as time went by, the lads were issued with shopper cycles so that they could nip ahead and cover the ground and carry more than a small pair of arms would embrace. Even when Watts entered the motorized age in 1915, buying a two-ton Selden to supplement their horses, the lads and their bikes were still very much a part of the crew.

John Watts had brought both his sons into the business, the younger, Arthur, riding the spare trace horse out to meet the heavily laden Beverley-bound cart as early as the age of eight. Arthur had gone over to France in the army during the First World War and hadn't really wanted to come back home to Beverley but, learning how his father wasn't in the best of health, he and elder brother William

literally took over the reins of the Watts carrying business in 1919. The taste of travel abroad had obviously opened Arthur's eyes to other ways of life beyond the confines of the Beverley-Hull carrying route. Whilst brother William was gifted in being able to make and produce with his hands, Arthur was the one with vision and the drive to improve their lot. That sole mechanized Selden apart, little had changed in the business of J. Watts, Carrier, for over 40 years, so they adopted a new title of Watts Bros and set out to make their mark.

Little could be done overnight to transform affairs but with first another Selden and then a De Dion three-tonner coming a couple of years later, the haulage side of the business was slowly expanded. Getting jobs for both the horses and the motorized vehicles, Arthur took the unusual step of going out on his push bike to tout for work. It was on one of these forays that he learnt of plans to develop the roads in the East Riding and how the authorities were looking for teams of workmen to undertake the contracts.

This construction programme was to be quite extensive. Not only were the cart tracks going to be upgraded to withstand the heavier motor cars, but what substantial roads had been laid were to be widened so that vehicles travelling in opposite directions could pass each other in comfort. This was deemed to be quite a luxury when the normal procedure of old had been for opposing carriages to slow almost to a halt, drivers lifting their hats as they squeezed past each other.

Although it was a type of job of which they had no experience whatsoever, Arthur got quite excited about the proposed developments and his enthusiasm was to win Watts Bros some hefty work, although whether they would be able to do it or not was going to be another matter. Whilst movement of materials was to be from a series of railheads, limiting the road transport to something like three-mile radius, it was to be in the speed of thi movement and in reducing handling time that Watts wer to excel. Whilst horses, carts and manpower were cheap, ii plentiful supply and the normal tools for this type of job the brothers invested £2,000 cash to buy their first Saure three-way tipper. The vehicle could handle six tons o roadstone, a weight that was totally impossible by traditional methods. The added bonus was that the vehicle could tip its contents mechanically either to the rear or the side so unloading time was just a slice of the normal handballing method.

The Watts road men became the talk of the region and, as the incoming revenue allowed, a further four Saurer tippers were bought for the same line of work. The road programme naturally stretched away from their Beverley base so, to ensure efficiency, Watts built some traditional living vans that were hooked up behind the Saurers. Parked up at the site of operations, they became home for the travelling Watts staff and their families.

By 1928, records show that a big transformation had taken place since the brothers had taken control. Watts Bros then had 27 employees on the payroll with nine heavy motor vehicles altogether in the business. Headquarters were still at Lairgate but with foresight the brothers had converted the original house and courtyard. By roofing it over, they not only created a garage but also the first loading stands for warehousing or transhipping between vehicles. Arthur Watts had equipped the place with electric light in 1923 and there was also underground storage for 1,500 gallons of petrol. John Watts had died in 1926 but his sons went on developing his earlier business through controlled expansion. Household removals became more prevalent and by 1932 the first custom-built removals van

50

Fleet number 4 was the first Saurer us[ed] by Watts, the three-way tipper costi[ng] £2,000 when bought new in 1922. With [a] capacity of six tons, the vehicle w[as] acquired specifically for a road-maki[ng] contract which launched Watts towar[ds] further success.

Following excellent service from the[ir] quartet of tippers, Watts Bros specified [a] Saurer chassis for this early example of [a] removals and general carrier vehicle. Y[O] 1788 was delivered in November 1932, [its] coachbuilt body displaying unasham[ed] indulgence in design and livery, with tack[le] boxes built in just above the lower skirt lin[e].

still based on the favoured Saurer chassis – was brought into use. This vehicle could also be used for a multitude of other roles, and that, in essence, was the Watts Bros formula for answering the transport needs of the area round Hull and Beverley.

In 1939, elder brother William decided to retire but the trading name of Watts Bros was retained, albeit with the words 'Proprietor: Arthur Watts' added underneath in small print. William's son George was to join the company, rising from the post of cycle delivery lad to Manager and Director responsible for the day-to-day running of the fleet as Arthur found his time taken up in a number of different ways. He

had entered the local council in 1934 and for five consecutive years filled the role of Mayor, with his wife as Mayoress. Such service to the community was recognized in 1947 when the town conferred the Freedom of the Borough upon them both. The strong bond with Beverley and the tradition of transport service given to the area was if anything strengthened during the Second World War. Even the growing postwar tentacles of British Road Services were fought off, although the constraint of a 25-mile operating radius had to be endured for the three years of effective nationalization.

One lasting effect BRS did have on the Watts business

By the late 1940s, general haulage was the predominant activity for Watts. This view inside the Manor Road garage reveals a substantial load of bagged British Sugar on board the 1945-vintage Maudslay Mogul dropsider. But it is the 1943 Atkinson six-wheeler that the current General Manager Chris Watson remembers best, for this Gardner-powered flat served Watts for 30 years before it was sold off in 1973. It is believed that this Atky is still alive and well and living somewhere on Humberside.

was to convince Arthur to change his livery. He had long favoured a pleasing red colour scheme but the Road Haulage Executive had virtually monopolized that sort of paintwork as their own, and Watts decided that he didn't want his fleet confused with the one run by the Government. In opting for an entirely different maroon and grey, he selected a livery which was still in use 40 years on.

Watts had strong views about not paying to advertise his Company's services: he always said that he preferred to let his vehicles speak for the firm. Doing so much multi-drop work in all the major settlements between Hull, Scarborough and York, the vehicles were a regular sight to many people. They were to become a positive tourist attraction when the vans' livery was changed to incorporate a huge map listing all the places they visited on a regular basis. The result of this ploy was that very few people would ever forget looking at a Watts vehicle. In fact, tales are told of some other wagon drivers receiving instructions on how to reach a particular place, the directions having been given from the map on the back of a Watts.

Some long-distance work was being done by 1957 when

Watts Bros went Limited, the directors being Arthur, his wife and nephew George. For his fleet flagships, Arthur ignored the current trend and stuck to the type of vehicle he preferred. Although there was nothing unusual about a predominance of Bedford and Commer four-wheelers for the lightweight multi-drop traffic, the heavyweight range saw Thornycroft eight-wheelers specified right up to the time of their disappearance into the AEC empire.

By the early 1960s, Watts Bros had firmly established its working pattern. Although the fleet was not more than 30 in number, all vehicles were kept extremely busy, especially in multi-drop distribution. Whilst the tipper work had been wound down, the removals side of the business had taken off. Storage depositories had become more important with more than 163,000 square feet of warehousing being brought into use. By now, Lairgate had long been outgrown and the thriving operations were now based at Manor Park. When John Watts had bought the farm on the outskirts of Beverley it had simply been a place where his horses could be grazed. Little did he realize how important this huge chunk of land would be to his descendants.

His great grandson, Chris Watson, the son of one of Arthur's three daughters, had come into the business in 1959. But the very complexity of the Watts family tree meant the company wasn't really amenable to being passed on. With such a high profile in the area, Watts Bros had received many enquiries about possible take-overs. In the end, it was Bill Revell whose approach convinced Arthur to sell up. In 1973, Revell was the Area Manager of a company called British Fuels Ltd, a relatively new concern having as its two shareholders The National Coal Board and Amalgamated Anthracite Holdings Ltd. The main aim for British Fuels was to buy up other well established, ongoing operations to allow its shareholders to diversify away from their main fuel interests. These newly acquired businesses would retain their individual autonomy and it was this directive that attracted Arthur Watts. The fact that the jobs of his staff would be safeguarded was perhaps the biggest wish of the 82-year-old and with that endorsed, the assets

Opposite: this 1947 Austin three-way-loader, the only one Watts operated, didn't have the best of reputations. But it wasn't to be left out when the fleet underwent a change of livery in about 1952 so that the old Watts red would not be confused with that of the BRS vehicles then dominating the road-haulage scene. The vehicle worked most of its days on static duties at the stand in Mytongate, Hull.

Above left: this Leyland Comet with fork trailer was Watts' first long-distance trunk vehicle, contracted to bring Lyons Tea back to Beverley from London for onward distribution. The outfit was bought as a

Opposite: one day in August 1954, the photographer catches three of the Watts fleet in Lairgate, Beverley, out of the 23 vehicles being operated at the time. Tom Walker is seen in bib-and-brace overalls beside Colin Banton and one of the company's two Jensens. This 1947 six-tonner with aluminium chassis has an odd drop-well body which could have been converted into a van, like its sister vehicle, had Watts wanted to change its use.

The Watts lorry gradually evolved into something rather several. The extended map of the East Riding highlights the Beverley Bar with the legend 'The Gateway to Yorkshire Distribution'. Arthur's aim of making his vehicles into head-turners certainly succeeded. Both tourists and other lorry drivers on invasion used the Watts maps to find their way around Yorkshire.

Arthur Watts always showed a rather nonconformist approach in his choice of workhorses, right from the earliest days when he bought French and Swiss vehicles to follow the first American one. Later, Thornycrofts were bought to head the fleet, this Mastiff of 14 tons gross capacity dating from 1961. Pictured in front of the celebrated Beverley Minster, the vehicle has lightweight Cravens Homalloy bodywork.

Above left: this Leyland Comet with York trailer was Watts' first long-distance trunk vehicle, contracted to bring Lyons Tea back to Beverley from London for onward distribution. The outfit was bought as a permanent combination, though the semi-trailer was to stay in service for 20 years. The practice of naming customers on the body sides was unique to this vehicle and had one drawback in that new companies were continually having to be added as new contracts were added to the Watts portfolio.

The Watts livery gradually evolved into something rather special. The extended map of the East Riding highlights the Beverley Bar with the legend 'The Gateway to Prompt Distribution' in flowing script. Arthur's aim of making his vehicles into head-turners certainly succeeded – both tourists and other lorry drivers on occasion used the Watts map to find their way around Yorkshire.

and goodwill of Watts Bros Ltd were signed over.

With George Watts retiring at the age of 65 in 1976, Eric Bilton came to Watts to take over as General Manager. Coming from the Grimsby Express Packet Co – another constituent company of British Fuels – he brought a knowledge of dock work that was soon taken on board by the Watts fleet. Bilton retired in 1990 and he was succeeded by Chris Watson, promoted from his post of Assistant General Manager. Watson is now at the helm of a fleet of

about 50 vehicles which is split fairly evenly between distribution and general haulage. A change in its parent's structuring about 1986 saw Watts Bros Ltd hived off with other non-fuel concerns under the umbrella of AAH Ltd. This move had little effect on the Watts business, but another development heralds the biggest transformation in the company's century-plus of history.

The modern distributor sees goods move through his hands in high volume. Although some material may sit in

Early one Sunday morning during 1962, Arthur Watts arranged for the entire fleet to go into Beverley for this memorable gathering. The 1943 Atkinson, fourth from left, suddenly seems rather out of place. Only one tipper was still in service by then, the Bedford 'S' type at the far right. Arthur's big Rover in the foreground indicates his position in the company, whilst the ex-GPO Morris 8 van hiding at the other end of the line of cars was being used by his grandson Chris Watson.

After a period of dominance by Bedford and Commer, it is now Leyland and ERF which are favoured for the four-wheeler van side of the Watts fleet. Number 116 is one of the latest ERF E6s to go into service, with a Ratcliffe tail-lift fitted to the body built by Stephensons of Hull. The vehicle has four doors fitted to its nearside, making life easier for its regular driver John Smith. His normal work pattern takes him to Lancashire on multi-drop distribution.

the warehouse for many months, a rapid turnaround is more usual and Watts Bros, like many, specialize in receiving bulk shipments and breaking them down into small orders. Within days, the goods are off again in smaller vehicles for their final delivery to places like supermarkets. It had long been realized that as a hub for this sort of operation, Beverley is not ideally located. Protracted and methodical planning is due to come to fruition in April 1991 (after this is written) when Watts Bros will move their base of operations some 25 miles south-westwards to Goole.

Arthur Watts died, aged 97, in 1988, having spent his last days in his bungalow home in the centre of what had been his life-long business. Though technically he no longer had any say in the company's policy, the impending move must have seemed an enormous upheaval to him: but he was realist enough to know that, if Watts Bros were to survive and prosper, the move out to Goole, alongside the motorway network, was long overdue, and to see it as a sign of hope for the future. It's a hope that all followers of classic road hauliers will share.

7: Marley Transport Ltd

Unless you work within Marley PLC, it may be difficult to grasp how big an international organization it is and how diverse a product range it has developed during its 66-year history. But the Marley Company of today first exploded on to the business scene and is probably still best known for its roof tiles, a product that its distinctive fleet of fine-liveried vehicles still hauls, day in and day out. Marley Transport Ltd, a wholly-owned subsidiary of Marley PLC, has its headquarters at Lichfield Road, Branston, near Burton-upon-Trent. Although it is currently run as an independent haulage contractor, its main priority is the delivery of the products of three sister companies: Marley Roof Tile Co Ltd, Marley Paving Ltd and Marley Building Systems Ltd. The smallest vehicle in the fleet of Marley Transport is a 30-ton (gross) rigid eight-wheeler, and it is thus apparent that there are many trucks owned and operated by the Marley organization that do not come under the specific umbrella of Marley Transport Ltd. But trucks, like tiles, have always been a part of Marley since the days when Owen Aisher senior decided to make his own roof tiles out of sand and cement because there was such a dire shortage of traditional ones made in clay.

In 1924, Aisher was already in business as a builder. He also made wooden doors and window frames for others in the profession, his trading name being The Marley Joinery Works – 'Marley' is an old Kentish name dating back to Pilgrim days. The purchase of a single Winget hand-operated roof tile press and the subsequent sale of its produce was destined to transform affairs. The fact that Aisher's letter-heads were quickly changed, with the word 'Tile' inserted in place of 'Joinery', illustrates how the door and window trade soon became redundant. Producing a cement tile didn't in itself take the building world by storm, for in fact most builders preferred clay tiles when they could get them. So to make his product more desirable, Aisher created a supply-and-fix business where complete

house roofs were supplied and fitted, entirely by Marley staff, at an agreed price.

With this extra, unique service, the Marley Tile laid its claim to acceptancy. By 1928, three works were in operation: the original base at Harrietsham in Kent, Storrington in Sussex and Leighton Buzzard in Bedfordshire. The first form of mass production was already instigated as the formula for Marley Tiles was quickly established. All that was needed was an ample supply of sand, cement and people – the first two to make a tile and the last to use it. Involved in the movement of his materials both before and after the production process, Aisher relied on the thoroughbreds of transport. Though it was the twilight of the steamer, heavyweight versions of both Foden and Garrett hauled sand and cement in and took tiles out.

From 1934, the tile business was to expand nationally. What prompted the development was a difference of opinion between Owen Aisher junior – who, along with brothers Dick and Jack, was working under their father – and Arthur Blackman who had co-founded the original joinery business with Owen senior. The matter was resolved by Blackman leaving, with a huge increase to his original investment as the Marley Tile (Holding) Company Ltd went public. Marley quickly opened more factories at Riverhead near Maidstone, Kent; Aveley in Essex; Burton-upon-Trent; Poole in Dorset and, in 1939, at Glasgow. Transport expanded in proportion and, as the new generation of diesel-propelled multi-wheelers ousted the steamers to the scrap heap, Marley took to AEC Mammoth Majors – both six- and eight-wheelers – operating them under a separate concern known as Tile Haulage Ltd.

The manufacture and transport of tiles both ceased during the war years as the Marley factories and vehicles were passed over to the war effort. Building concrete barges and sections of the famous Mulberry Harbour were just me of their varied activities. The demand for such things evaporated when peace was declared in 1945, but what the war had shown Marley was that they could turn their hands to almost anything. They continued in this vein in peacetime as prefabricated houses, sectional buildings, floor tiles and plastics became more and more important to the expanding Marley organization. Roof tiles had come back into strong production too, and new factories were opened at Beenham near Reading and Delamere in Cheshire. But it was another site, near Ebchester in County Durham, opened in 1953, which was to achieve particular notoriety among the people in the Marley Transport organization.

Although the hire and reward sector of the transport industry was to undergo the nightmare of nationalization, this didn't affect own-account operations. Strangely, Marley first opted for a different tactic in postwar transport in that the Aisher family created their own separate haulage company known as Martin & Sillett Ltd. During the period of total government acquisition of long-distance haulage, the vehicles were run by Marley Tiles under 'C' hiring licences, thus avoiding compulsory purchase. Martin & Sillett Ltd were eventually brought into the main Marley

building concern of Aytons. But what makes the plant remarkable in road haulage terms is the incline of its approach roads: the gradient of the fearsome Chair Bank is reckoned to be an alarming 1 in 6. It's a hefty enough climb in the 1990s – 30 or 40 years ago it was a nightmare, and one the Marley men of the day, with 24 tons gross on their backs, had to surmount every time they left the factory.

Being so far north away from the administrative HQ in Kent meant that the fleet of 12 or 15 multi-wheelers based at Ebchester were very often hand-me-downs, with the old S18 Fodens used well on into the 1960s. The spec of this type of vehicle makes interesting reading. No heater, of course, and with so many water leaks from the system, anti-freeze was never used so draining was a nightly chore during the winter. The Fodens of that era were well known for their braking system which had the normal hydraulic line pressure boosted by an engine-driven pump – fine in theory, but if the engine stalled you were virtually brakeless on a vehicle that didn't have foundation brake units fitted to the second steering axle. A single windscreen wiper was standard and it was considered quite a perk if the mechanics fitted a second one to give some vision through the nearside

Before setting up the Marley Tile business, Owen Aisher traded as a builder and contractor. FY 2141 is an example of the Foden five-tonner which was first produced in 1905. The type was built to conform to the 1904 Heavy Motor Car Order which allowed for 20 ton gross 'wagon and drag' outfits – 12 tons for the wagon plus up to eight tons on a trailer. The Foden was 6ft 6in wide and had a top speed of 15mph. This particular vehicle was Foden number 7820, produced in 1917 for the War Department and then sold off in the surplus sales of 1920.

organization but up until the advent of 'O'-licensing in 1968, the M & S name was still used with 'C' carriers' licences. A pattern for the tile wagons was soon established. Although administered totally from Riverhead, the fleet was based at the various depots in the day-to-day control of staff on site. A centralized buying policy saw Gardner-powered Foden and Atkinson eight-wheeled flats adopted as standard, but their performance parameters were always measured by a visit to Ebchester.

The Newlands factory at Ebchester is situated over the river from the village in the county of Northumberland, Marley having bought the original sand quarry from the

half of the split windscreen.

Providing the propulsion was the revered Gardner 6LW engine which had a reputation for reliability and long life but never one for speed. With only 112bhp on tap, you had less than 5bhp per ton and progress up the Chair fully loaded didn't even reach a good walking pace. Ironically, once you reached the main A694 road in Ebchester itself there was a large 'Slow' sign at the T-junction – but at least you didn't have to stop right on the peak. There was no chance to speed up, however, for the main Marley route for southbound loads then turned left and headed upwards again, with Station Bank to contend with next.

Steam wagons gathered at Storrington are, left to right, a 1930 Garrett six-wheeled tipper TL 1494, fleet no 16; a 1927 Foden six-wheel artic PX 6839, fleet no 5; a 1926 Foden artic KM 5943, fleet no 1; and another 1930 Garrett, PO 1471, which was fleet no 15. Left: for legal reasons this 1927 Foden artic, works number 12654, registered KO 3290, was referred to as a 'flexible six-wheeler'. Photographed after a repaint in 1934, the 'C' type chassis is linked to a 23ft trailer, the combination being capable of taking a 10-ton load. Contrary to modern practice, this trailer wasn't easily detachable from the tractor unit, although the trailer axle could be made to steer for tight manoeuvres.

The Chair was short and sharp, but Station Bank was slightly less sharp – the gradient varies around the 1 in 8 mark – but far, far longer. The Marley men reckoned on taking at least 20 minutes just to reach the Hat & Feather and the start of the run down into Leadgate which was hardly four miles out from their factory gates.

Whilst this may have been a regular, acceptable chore for the Ebchester-based staff, the Marley drivers who came from other far-flung depots found the experience simply frightening. If they managed to get a loaded vehicle into Newlands without using one of the many escape lanes on Station Bank it was deemed to be good driving. Some of them then needed the help of an Ebchester fitter to instruct them how to find crawler bottom when they insisted that their Fodens couldn't climb the hill out from the plant. It wasn't a lack of skill, it was just that all the time they had driven the wagon before they had never needed to whip out of the normal bottom gear, lift the lever-mounted clip then push the gearstick over and back into that house-end-climbing ratio.

It was normal practice to get into crawler at the bottom of the Chair. For the unwary visitors who went to snatch it at a midway point, the whole heart-jerking episode normally ended with the vehicle's propshaft in tatters and the only

concern then was to make a dignified retreat. But if you did stay in one piece, another sound piece of Ebchester advice was to rack back the Gardner's pump: the excess fuel allowed through gave a touch more power and of course a terrific smoke-screen to hide your progress.

Whilst this type of vehicle and performance may have been the norm in the mid-1950s for everyone in transport, it was still usual for Marley in the mid and late 1960s as these same 6LW-powered Fodens continued to be run. True, they received a regular two-year overhaul back at Riverhead, but with millions of miles under their belts they were only kept on the road by hard-working fitting staff out in the field. As the Marley Group went from strength to strength, diversifying round the globe, their roof-tile wagons were just run until they stopped and the running was done at a very slow pace.

Ralph Taylorson, now a dedicated Ebchester-based Marley driver, is one for whom the old Marley Fodens in the 1960s were a well remembered sight. At that time Ralph worked for the famous heavy-haulage concern of Siddle C. Cook and, carrying all sorts of out-of-gauge loads, he often found himself thumbing a lift home with his wagon having to be parked up early in the day. Seeing a Marley Tile wagon approach meant he could get a lift close to his

Although originally permitted legally in 1930 to allow the steamers to hang on to a niche in the transport market-place, the concept of an eight-wheeled vehicle was to transform the road-haulage scene. AEC were the first to produce a factory-built eight-wheeler with internal-combustion engine, in early 1934. This quartet of Mammoth Majors dates from 1936 and Marley Tile followers will quickly spot the early use of the distinctive side-mounted, embossed fleet numbers. The eight-leggers were limited to 22 tons gross, but the high side boards meant they could carry sand in bulk as well as tiles. Below: Atkinson and Foden eight-wheeled rigids were the backbone of the Marley Tile fleet throughout the 1950s and '60s. Number 146 dated from 1960 and, with the Gardner 6LX engine and David Brown six-speed gearbox, it was rated as quite a flyer, having a top speed close to 48mph. Seen in the British Steel works on Teesside during 1964, it is waiting for sheets over a load of crushed slag. The roof-mounted reflective sign was a standard fitment of the era: made up of small round glass 'fruit gums', it rattled profusely when the engine was ticking over.

Fleet number 126 was also photographed on Teesside in 1964, its bagged slag load destined for an experimental tile-making process which Marley did not pursue. The 1964 Atkinson was rated at 20 tons gross and was powered by a 6LW engine. The single-axle semi-trailer with skeleton side boards was known as a roofing-felt trailer because that material was carried in bulk on these outfits which took a 13-ton payload. Trailers of this pattern were built by both Merriworth and Taskers.

Consett base but Ralph recalls that he preferred to try and hide, hoping the Marley driver wouldn't see him, as such a ride back would be far too slow – and that was coming from an old Scammell man!

But the 1970s brought a big change for Marley Transport. In 1970, the name actually embraced three divisions: Roof Tile Haulage, Warehousing & Box Van distribution, and a Contract Hire Division which looked after their own cars, vans and even ran a vehicle hire business. The decade was to herald a new look in tile vehicles as Ford D-series were tried, not very successfully, and a return made to AEC in place of Foden and Atkinson. Even having the latter marque powered by the Gardner 6LX-150 engine didn't produce enough power, and mechanic Cliff Hedley recalls fitting bigger springs in the governor box so that the top speed was lifted to a more respectable 55mph.

With the new generation of AECs, in contrast, it was a case of having to derate their 12-litre 760 engines just to slow them down, as 80mph was a speed well within the capability of the lightweight Marshal Major six-wheelers. Running at 24 tons gross, the 1970s six-wheeler could carry

the same payload as a 1950s eight-wheeler. The law had been changed to allow for a 30-ton gross eight-wheeler but it was not being able to lift and stack roof tiles any higher than two tiers on a fixed body-length which limited the amount of payload. The introduction of artics into the tile fleet, with 40ft trailers, obviously did allow for more tiles to be carried, up to the 32-ton limit. But that class of vehicle was a nightmare if it was destined for the depths of quagmire that building sites were famous for.

Handballing roof tiles had been standard practice ever since 1924, and lifting four or at most five tiles a time either up and on to your vehicle or down and off was a back-breaking job. There could be 4,000 tiles on a 32-tonner, so doing this day in, day out didn't instill a great deal of driver enthusiasm. One Marley driver recalled that he always handled tiles with his back turned to what was left on his lorry so he didn't continually see how many more tiles were left to shift. But the driver's lot was set to improve. Whilst the AEC marque was replaced first by Leyland Bisons and Buffalos – recalled for an ability to go like hell but then blow up – a long-term trial with a Volvo F86 demonstrator, naturally at Ebchester, signposted a direction that the

ter successful early trials with the Volvo
6, this Swedish marque quickly came to
ake up the majority of the Marley
ransport fleet, and the F7 eight-wheeled
gid is still much in evidence. In this Paul
cNally photograph, Alan Gibb is seen
out to leave his Carluke base in about
86, his load consisting of three sectional
rages made by Marley Building Systems.
arluke later ceased production and its
ve-vehicle fleet – this F7, a six-wheeler
d three artics – were transferred to other
epots around the country.

ompany has followed for the last 15 years. This new
wedish marque soon got great driver acceptance. But the
roblem of handling the tiles wasn't remedied as easily, as
Managing Director Geoff Lampard recalled.

He and Eric Hughes had been tasked with easing this
andling difficulty. An early idea to shrink-wrap in small
acks brought complaints from the far-flung depots of the
oad moving far too easily. Geoff decided to see for himself
nd from Ebchester he took out a fully loaded Ford six-
heeler for a delivery in Newcastle. The V8 Perkins
owered him down the Low Road with no problems but
negotiating the first roundabout he came to at Whickham
aw the whole top stack of tiles slide sideways. Geoff,
nowever, was blessed with double good fortune in that all

the tiles were caught in the securing net and an adjacent
pub car park allowed him to stop off the road and consider
his dilemma. With tiles sticking out in all directions, the
situation could only be made worse as the next person to
drive on to the car park was a police motor cyclist. His
quizzical look at the Ford's load prompted Lampard to
remark, 'We always carry our tiles like this.' The attempt at
a joke didn't melt much ice as the officer reached for his
book and pointed out the offence of not securing a load
properly. 'Is it actually an offence whilst I'm on a pub car
park?' asked Lampard, extremely sharp thinking in the
circumstances. The law man reluctantly agreed that as long
as he stayed in the car park, in that form, then he couldn't
be booked.

With the announcement of the T45 range
of Scammell-built Constructor 8s, Marley
took one on long-term appraisal but it
didn't impress as much as the Volvo. At
the Riverhead factory near Sevenoaks, the
operator is demonstrating how a roof-tile
grab can be used to lift palleted loads with
a set of slings. The Riverhead plant was to
close in 1988 and NKO 276W was sold to R.
B. Sentence, a roofing contractor from
Essex.

Another different commodity regularly hauled by the fleet was Marley Mix. Driver Mark Kember is here supervising the loading of his F7 during 1983 at Aveley, South Ockendon, in Essex. The cargo is destined for delivery around the DIY merchants in London and this multi-drop work was a big headache with a product that had to be kept completely dry until used. Marley Mix is no longer produced and the Aveley factory now concentrates on paving.

Getting to grips, literally, with roof tiles took a long time to sort out. Whilst the Hiab type of grab was already in use to handle loads like bricks, the main problem for Marley was to find a grab to hold tiles which, if not handled properly, could easily be damaged. But, by 1980, the end of handballing was in sight and a big investment programme took place as the eight-wheelers on fleet were all fitted with either centrally-mounted standard-boom or rear-mounted long-boom cranes.

In 1981, Marley, a company who continually reassess themselves, put the transport arm back into the melting pot. The three divisions instigated in 1970 were scrapped: distribution and warehousing went back into the original Marley Companies that had created them and the vehicle service hire part was formed into Marley Vehicle Leasing Ltd. The roof-tile haulage division was thus able to take the name Marley Transport Ltd and it was Geoff Lampard who was given the role of Managing Director in 1983. The last seven years under Lampard's control have seen big changes in Marley Transport Ltd. The concept of 38 tonnes on five

With the advent of regulations allowing 38-tonne artics, Marley Transport opted for the Volvo F12 to head a 2+3 configuration at the new weight band. Burton-based A659 HVT is seen brand-new in October 1983 having just been given into the care of regular driver Terry Frost. Terry, who has been with this haulier for 25 years, has since clocked up over half a million miles with this Volvo. It is coupled to a York tri-axle semi-trailer which carries an Atlas Roll-crane, here handling a load of paving bricks.

arley continued to buy the F7 whilst it
as the only model offered by Volvo as a
,id eight-wheeler but, with the
nnouncement of the FL10, this more
werful variant became their standard
oice. This example has just been
livered to the depot at Sawston,
mbridgeshire, in March 1989. The
erator is seen moving a pack of Anglia
of tiles which weigh 1.2 tonnes. The
hicle is fitted with a Hiab 100 long-boom
ane and Probust grab.

les was quickly accepted, with a 2+3 configuration,
ampard opting for the Volvo F12 as his premium work-
orse. Distribution to more destinations with hard standing
ow means the artic plays an important role at Marley and
quipping as required with Roll Loader cranes also allows a
elf-unloading facility.

Marley Transport Ltd now has a road fleet which is
00% Volvo, with maintenance carried out either at five of
heir 10 depots or where applicable at an adjacent Volvo
ealership. A flexible, eight-year replacement programme
or the 100+ vehicles now sees new machinery regularly
oming on the road. And, a big change to yesteryear, there

is always a queue of prospective purchasers waiting for
Marley cast-offs. There has also been a change in drivers'
attitudes, with the quality of esprit de corps being
something that Marley Transport actively encourages.
Issuing drivers with a mix-and-match type of uniform for
them to wear as they pilot some of the best machinery on
the road, equipped with the latest in mechanical handling
devices, has produced a big change from the image of, say,
25 years ago. No longer do people hide at the sight of a
Marley vehicle, and the enthusiasm of the staff for
attending events like Truckfest is regularly rewarded with
trophies reflecting the excellent standard of this fleet.

f you travel round the truck shows, you
will see the Marley Transport fleet as
egular exhibitors. These aren't the same
vehicles and crews each time, simply
volunteers from the depot nearest to any
particular event. Affectionately known as
'F' troop, this quintet of Ebchester-based
vehicles were captured in May 1990 prior to
retaining their award for the Best Working
Fleet at the Geordie Truckers' Show. Left
to right are Kevin Roberts (and assistant),
Alan Fairless, Ralph Taylorson, Derek
Greaves and traffic office man Paul
McNally.

8: Blue Circle Cement

It is always difficult to quantify the value of a name. Whilst marketing people sometimes spend huge budgets to conjure up new images, it is often the case that the simplest of concepts somehow easily wins through. A case in point is the name Blue Circle: although it is now the banner of a diverse international organization, it remains synonymous for most people with the cement industry. Brigadier-General Critchley is credited with the first use of the blue circle symbol in the marketing of cement round about 1920. But the story of the company really goes back to 1900 when, not for the first time, a co-operative approach salvaged an industry that was close to strangling itself.

Historically, the area of North Kent has always been the heartland of British cement production. During the 19th century, huge numbers of concerns had set themselves up in business following the Aspdin patent of Portland Cement in 1824. This type of cement was a more durable product than the traditional cement mix, taking its name from its colour, when dry, which resembled Portland Stone. Whilst competition is normally deemed to be good for business, in the 1890s an excess of competitors using close to 1,000 bottle kilns in cement-making was meaning low profitability, thus no investment in newer production methods. The situation screamed out for an amalgamation of interests which finally occurred when the so called 'share pusher' financier Henry Osborne O'Hagan pulled together 26 diverse concerns under the umbrella of The Associated Portland Cement Manufacturers (1900) Ltd.

After a rather rocky start to affairs, matters improved when APCM created as a subsidiary The British Portland Cement Manufacturers Ltd in 1911. This latter concern eventually drew the bigger names of G. & T. Earle and I.C. Johnson into the organization which was known locally as 'the combine'. Strangely, it wasn't until 1920 that the concept of marketing a single brand of Portland Cement – Blue Circle – under the single administration of the Cement

Marketing Company Ltd, was introduced. Prior to that, excess of 50 different brand names were competing again each other to sell what was really a very similar product.

The one exception to the single-brand rule was G. & T Earle of Hull who, until the 1960s, continued to use the own name and marketing department although still i essence part of the APCM organization. Earle apart, t Cement Marketing Company was now a base to be bui upon and although there were still many other independer producers, Blue Circle was destined to become a househol name for cement both here and abroad.

For distribution purposes, CMC were to adopt thre specific methods covering sea, rail and road, and with clos integration they all operated well together. For roa vehicles, APCM had bought their first Atkinson six-tonne in 1916, which was in essence the first year in tru production of the new Lancashire manufacturer. Thi model of Atkinson was to be bought in great numbers unt 1928 when the Preston company ceased building steam propelled vehicles. Rather than opt for a total change to th internal-combustion engine range, CMC then started to bu the Sentinel Super steamer model, fleet numbers 100, 10 and 104 being pneumatic-tyred 10-ton capacity six-wheeler which came into service in 1928. Looking back, it may seer difficult to understand why CMC continued to rui steamers. At the time, however, their reputation fo strength was unrivalled, an ideal asset for such a heav product as cement. In fact, even though the famous DC Foden range – with fleet numbering in the 300s – came inte use about 1938, the 100-series of Sentinels weren't finall pensioned off until the early 1950s.

During the war years the steamers proved to be a godsend, giving their best performance on an anthracit type of Welsh coal. Preparation time with the Sentinel always meant a rather leisurely start to the day waiting fo pressure to build up in the boiler. But at least this wa

edictable, unlike the conversions carried out on some
N5 petrol-engined Commers. To save fuel, they were
ed to run on producer gas during the war and it was
called that it could take an hour to wind them up just to
oduce a miserly performance.

The years from 1939 to 1945 saw everyone in the country
us their attention on priorities for the war effort and
MC were no exception. The early 1930s had at least
ought them some stability when negotiation with other
g concerns like Tunnel and Rugby Cement had brought
out a common price agreement. The 1930s also first saw
ment moved in paper sacks, but by June 1940 the
eviously used jute sacks were back in use and both CMC
ivers and customers were implored to return their empty
te sacks as paper ones were in very short supply.
owever, many people found that if they boiled the jute
ck long enough the Blue Circle emblem would disappear.
hus many cement sacks were to end their days stuffed
ith down and used as pillow cases.

Wartime hire and reward road haulage was coordinated
der the auspices of the Ministry of War Transport

1940s naturally saw a great demand for their produce, first
for military installations and then in peacetime years to
rebuild all the damage that had been done during the war.

Another battle that APCM were to fight – along with all
the other cement people – in the late 1940s was against
nationalization. The postwar Labour government succeeded
with coal, electricity, gas, the railways and then partially in
road haulage but before cement was also swept up, the
Conservatives came back into power. 1951 signalled a
period when the cement makers could stop fending off this
attack on their livelihood and concentrate on doing what
they did best, making and distributing cement.

The 1950s also brought a gradual transition away from
100 years of standard practice: for all that time, cement had
been delivered in bags, whether paper or jute. Even the
ships that supplied far off places like Gateshead and
Glasgow from Swanscombe Works carried that precious
powder in bagged form. Three times a week one of the
'Wood' vessels – Westwood, Dalewood, Levenwood,
Cedarwood, Rosewood or Beechwood – came up to the
North-East to discharge directly into the Tyneside

tkinson steam wagons were the backbone of the Cement Marketing Company fleet until the Super Sentinels arrived in the late 1920s.
hotographed in 1920 after winning a concours competition run by *Commercial Motor* are three six-tonners. This model was Atkinson's
irst big success, manufactured at their premises in Kendal Street, Preston. Designed by 'Scotty Joe' Haythorn, the vehicle bore a strong
esemblance to the contemporary Sentinel. A big bonus with the early Atkinsons was the use of solid rubber tyres rather than the then-
ormal steel rims, giving a smoother ride. Selling price for a complete wagon and cab, painted as required, was £1,170.

MOWT), and CMC vehicles also found themselves taken
nto their control. A Dunstable driver like Henry Wraight
may have left home on a Monday morning with a relatively
ocal delivery of bagged cement but he probably then found
himself tramping country-wide with all sorts of traffic
under MOWT instruction and not getting back home until
a Friday night. The depot at Dunstable had actually
delivered as far away as Liverpool in the 1930s but three-
day treks like that were curtailed during the war. The
MOWT decreed that no cement should travel by road more
than 40 miles from any works so CMC introduced a system
of zoning to cut down on fuel and operating costs. The

warehouse. The cargo was slung back on to dry land in one-
ton batches, and if the ship had endured a rough ride up the
North Sea, it wouldn't be surprising if six out of every 20
one-hundredweight bags were burst open. The resulting
mess was put right by the use of a bagging machine where
the powder was filtered and rebagged prior to delivery. It
was a cement driver's dream to have a full load of nice clean
rebags without spillage.

Gateshead was an odd offshoot of the CMC organization
which was predominantly located in the south of England.
The South Shore warehouse had been built on land that
had been used in kiln production of cement by I.C.

Fodens began to be taken into serv[ice] during the late 1930s and remained [the] main CMC workhorse for the next thi[rty] years. Number 554 dates from 1947, [an] eight-ton version from the DG range, a[nd] is seen at the House of Commons – more [to] deliver a message than cement, by the lo[ok] of it. This vehicle was based [at] Hurlingham, a plant still in use by B[lue] Circle and nowadays serviced by t[wo] converted Rhine barges on the Tham[es.] These vessels shuttle bulk cement fro[m] Northfleet, both being fitted with eig[ht] separate pots each of which can carry 1[00] tonnes.

Blue Circle had to live with the threat [of] nationalization for nearly five years duri[ng] the late 1940s. Both vehicles and ba[gs] carried slogans against this proposal by t[he] Labour Government. CMC always like[d] the type of deep-skirted bodywo[rk] illustrated here because of the advertisi[ng] space it offered and the style was on[ly] dropped after 1968 when vehicles began [to] need more work on their undersides, part[ly] because of annual test requirement[s.] Number 656 was an AEC Mammoth datin[g] from 1948, the few that CMC ran bein[g] remembered for their smoothness and ver[y] low-geared steering.

1952, bulk movements by road were coming more prevalent, and these new 8 Fodens are seen loading at the unstable works. The FGs were fitted with malloy tipping bodies and could carry a ton load. The figure beside the rearward den is Albert Price, garage foreman at e Bedfordshire plant where the fleet rose a peak of 104 vehicles at one time. hough the silos are still in position, they e not now in use: Dunstable is currently distribution point and the base for just ve vehicles.

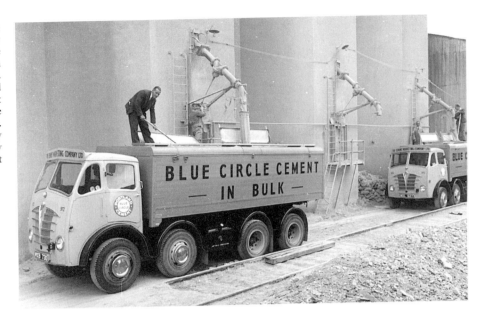

ohnsons in the 1890s. So far away from head office, the ad fleet at Gateshead had always been a strange mixture. ome solid-tyred Leyland four-wheelers were in use during he 1920s, whilst other prewar vehicles included a Sentinel-arner petrol-engined four-tonner. There was also a ulcan four-tonner and a trio of normal-control six-ton Commers which had their front axles set back under the ear of the engine. An early DG Foden six-wheeler came, ut having only a trailing axle in the rear bogie gave it ather poor performance.

The Sentinels were about at the end of their realistic life y 1950, as driver Jack Rawlinson would testify for he heared a stub axle at Warwick Bridge one day en route ack from Carlisle. The only way to get the vehicle mobile gain was to strip a similar Sentinel of the relevant parts

back at base and then rebuild the crashed vehicle at the roadside. The CMC had been virtually forced to get long life from their fleet by a mixture of wartime constraints and lengthy delivery times for new vehicles. To ensure a continued high standard for the enlarging fleet, they introduced a system of rebuilds performed at Beddington, a name which is really part of Blue Circle folklore.

After five years of life a vehicle was withdrawn from service, sent south to Beddington, near Croydon, and stripped right down to the chassis. The rebuild was from the first nut and bolt upwards. Before the scuttle was fitted, it wasn't unknown for the service staff to weld a message to the underside that wouldn't be read until five years later. When complete, the vehicle was put back into service, although it didn't always go back to the depot where it had

Number 1174 came new to Gateshead on September 21, 1954, and was given first to driver Jim Wilkinson as his regular steed. Jim recalls that the truck was fitted with a Redhill cab and in the winter there was often more frost inside than out. One interesting return trip from Carlisle had to be done in 'automatic' after the clutch pedal snapped. The 4LW-powered vehicle was returned to Beddington in 1958 to be fitted out as a bulk tanker.

Number 1387 is one of just two Albion Clydesdales which joined the fleet in 1956. With a Bonallock cab and lightweight body, its unladen weight was less than four tons, so it could carry loads like the 200 hundredweight sacks of cement shown here, 10 tons of cargo, within its 14 tons gross limit. It worked first out of Glasgow and wasn't very well appreciated by the Scottish drivers but, strangely, when it was posted down to Oxford, the men at that depot couldn't speak too highly of it.

first come from. Beddington also sourced all the brand new vehicles which were gradually to change in profile as the traditional bags gave way to various forms of bulk delivery. Tipping closed bodies were the first type, seen in the early 1950s, and pressure discharge pots and the novel Air Slide boxes were coming on to the scene soon after.

Carrying the new bodywork were mostly Foden and Leyland chassis, which in comparable performance were like chalk and cheese. The Foden-Gardner combination gave the CMC some excellent service but they could be exceptionally slow. The one bonus that Gateshead depot had was in fitter Eric Lewins who always seemed able to extract just a bit more go than usual from the Patricroft engine. The early Fodens also lacked a bit in stopping power. Jim Wilkinson can recall one day, dropping down into Brough with fleet no 322, a maturing 16-year-old

seven-tonner, registered EXF 322, when a break in the rear nearside hydraulic pipe saw him fly through the village with the handbrake fully ratcheted on and the engine screaming in low gear. Jim rang in to his Gateshead depot manager Sam 'Ossy' Kelly to report the problem: with the drop at Appleby only eight miles on, he said he would continue, using the gearbox and handbrake. With the load safely off, it was a case of adjusting up the handbrake again and a steady 70-mile ride back up to Tyneside.

Providing a good delivery service was all part of the CMC package. Being own-account people, the drivers were rewarded with perks like anti-freeze – unheard of on the hire and reward side – radiator muffs for the winter and good remuneration calculated on a fixed schedule with a 16mph average speed. Whilst that 16mph may have been just within the grasp of the loaded Fodens, the Leylands

When Jim Wilkinson had 1174 taken from him, he was given this Leyland Comet which went into service at Gateshead in January 1959. Fitted with a Carmichael tank and Godfrey blowing equipment, it was limited to a payload of less than seven and a half tons within its 14-ton limit. A notable few weeks away from the North-East for this vehicle came during the reconstruction of the A74 in the Dumfries area. It was Jim's job to keep the local contractors supplied with cement, shuttling from rail trucks in a siding at Lockerbie.

Although the CMC fleet during the 1950s and '60s was mainly a mix of Foden multi-wheelers and Leyland four-wheelers, lightweights like Bedfords and these Commer TS3s were also seen in service. Number 1735 dates from 1960 and is fitted with a Carmichael aluminium tank supported on a steel subframe and lifted by twin underarm tipping gear.

were recalled as flyers. But representations from Glasgow that their Fodens couldn't deal with their hilly catchment area meant that Gateshead were to lose their 'top gear' motors in exchange for some Scottish Fodens. So called because you hardly ever changed out of top gear, the Leyland Beaver four-wheelers were soon to be uprated to six-wheelers with the fitment of Boys third axles. They were also converted from platform to tank operation, and an example of this type has managed to survive into the preservation scene.

Not many of these heavy-duty Beavers came into service but the lighter Comets were ordered in droves. Many of these short-wheelbase four-wheelers were run in tank form, the blowing equipment being mounted inside the cab in the area normally taken up by the passenger seat. These CMC bulkers were able to self-load themselves and many of this type of vehicle worked from railheads, drawing the bulk cement from a line of CMC-owned rail trucks. Using the

lorry-mounted blower equipment it was a fairly simple matter to pipe compressed air across to the rail truck and then blow the cement via another pipe back to the road vehicle. Weight was always a critical matter to the CMC man but by tapping the side of his tank he could gauge what progress was being made inside. A look through the top hatch would confirm things and by the time he climbed back down to switch the blower off, the vehicle would be fully loaded. With good equipment, properly sealed, a ton a minute could be shifted as cement, when aerated, simply flows like water.

It was this property that CMC made use of in their Air Slide bulkers. An internal slope of 7 to 10 degrees was all that was needed to create movement once compressed air was bubbled into the powder. The principle is still in use in the current Blue Circle rail fleet, each of this type of wagon carrying about 37 tons of cement. However, for road use the Air Slide was limited to a ground hopper discharge point

It's only in the last decade that Blue Circle has been biased towards the use of articulated trucks, the rigid being preferred earlier because so much work took them onto inferior building-site roads. But number 2170 was an exception to that rule, coming into service during 1964. It had the Foden two-stroke engine mated to a five-speed plus super-low gearbox. The four-in-line running gear supporting the rear of the tank turned out to be something of a headache when a high level of braking efficiency began to be required to meet the annual testing legislation introduced in 1968.

About 1970, CMC switched to Scammell preference to Foden for their mul wheeled fleet, and they were to contin buying the Mk3 Routeman until the moc was replaced by the Constructor 8 arou 1981. This batch, which were known lightweights, went into service at t Cauldron works, fitted with 540cu ft tan and running at 24 tons gross. Wh changes in legislation allowed six-wheel rigids to run at that weight, these pressu tanks were remounted on Leyland Bis chassis. The twin hatches on the tan permitted loading at any of the 176 vario points then in use by Blue Circle.

and not really suitable for the higher-placed silos that were slowly coming into use.

The class of vehicle as well as the marque and size of it was a matter of policy that was decided upon by the Group Transport Engineer. Don Broomfield filled this role for many years and at his dictate the Beddington staff found themselves fitting more and more pressure discharge tanker bodies on to rigid chassis. Broomfield was well known for his lack of interest in the articulated outfit: the problems of traction on building sites were bad enough for a rigid, never mind an artic, especially when unladen.

Where good footing could be guaranteed, the artic was considered. Three such outfits came to Dunstable and were hardly ever off the motorway as their daily task was to keep the Birmingham depot fully supplied. Known by drivers as the 'Banana Boats', the Foden tractive units were heavy-duty 6x4s with the S21 cab and super-single tyres. Having the straight-six cylinder Cummins power pack, the outfits were amongst the fastest wagons of the day.

As well as the motorway age, the 1960s also brought an unprecedented demand for more and more cement. In 1961, Blue Circle even had to import the stuff to keep up supply

so a programme of expansion was quickly signalled. A ne plant at Dunbar, just round the coast from Edinburg opened in 1963, this works taking over the bulk supply depots at Grangemouth, Dundee, Inverness and Aberdee Strangely, the depots at Uddingston and Cambuslang o the outskirts of Glasgow were still supplied from works Kent. Shipment by sea to the North-East was to end 1966 when the Eastgate plant was opened, offering 600,000-ton capacity produced by two kilns operating o the semi-dry process. The rearrangement on Tyneside als saw the CMC fleet based here, around 30 vehicles at it high point, move out to a new depot at Heaton.

All the depots were to notice a big change in the ne vehicles coming into service at the end of the 1960s. A ever-changing specification was CMC's main complaint t the Sandbach manufacturer who had been the fleet's mai supplier for over 30 years, so in Foden's place the Scamme Routeman Mk 3 took over the mantle of fleet flagship Coming with a fairly short wheelbase, the first 40 bulker were run at a fairly modest 24 tons gross. It took some tim for the legislation covering the rigid eight-wheeler to catc up with the four-axled artic version, running at 32 tons, bu

The flexibility of articulation was th theme for the 1980s, and a total of 20 Leyland Roadtrain 4x2 tractive units wer commissioned. They were powered by th well-liked Rolls-Royce 265 engine and thei payload was standardized at 20 tons within the 32-ton limit. Number 2547A here displays the distinctive clean-cut new log as it unloads at Portrack on Teesside on June 9, 1986. The same type of 'banana tank is now run at the 38-tonne limit behind the Scammell-built three-axle tractive units which predominate in the fleet today.

Atkinson steam wagons sold to APCM Ltd and CMC Ltd 1916–1928

Makers' no	Reg no	Date	Company/fleet no	Disposal
12	CK 3005	Oct 1916	APCM – CMC 4	sold 1926
85	CK 3059	Aug 1918	APCM 2	scrapped 1929
132	CK 3120	Aug 1919	APCM – CMC 6	sold 1931
154	CK 3149	Oct 1919	APCM – CMC 7	sold 1929
168	CK 3201	Feb 1920	APCM – CMC 8	sold 1930
170	CK 3203	Feb 1920	APCM – CMC 9	scrapped 1931
176	CK 3210	Apr 1920	APCM	
185	CK 3229	Mar 1920	APCM 18 – CMC	sold 1926
196	CK 3249	Apr 1920	APCM 20 – CMC 11	sold 1929
200	CK 3251	May 1920	APCM 21 – CMC	sold 1925
204	CK 3257	May 1920	CMC 10	sold 1930
205	CK 3256	May 1920	CMC 11	
212	CK 3279	Jun 1920	Martin Earle – APCM – CMC (1925)	sold 1927
220	CK 3288	Jul 1920	APCM 22 – CMC 22	sold 1930
221	CK 3297	Jul 1920	APCM 23 – CMC 19	sold 1929
227	CK 3314	Jul 1920	APCM 24 – CMC 21	sold 1926
242	CK 3335	Sep 1920	CMC 13	
269	CK 3405	Mar 1921	CMC	sold 1927
490	YK 4969	Jun 1925	CMC 5	sold 1933
491	YK 7937	Jul 1925	CMC 40	sold 1934
495	YL 5656	Oct 1925	CMC	sold 1930
501	YM 2103	Jan 1926	CMC 18	sold 1933
502	YM 3257	Jan 1926	CMC 4	
508	YN 6983	Mar 1926	CMC 49	sold 1931
509	YP 2509	Jul 1927	CMC 3	
510	KL 3820	1925	CMC 33	
520	YE 8500	Mar 1927	CMC 21	sold 1933
521	YE 8499	Mar 1927	CMC 22	sold 1932

y the end of the 1970s the Scammells were running at the
0 tons gross mark.

With a fleet that was to peak around a total of 1,600 ehicles, including 750 Routemen in service during 1977, Blue Circle were still experiencing the occasional perational difficulty. Supply both in bagged and bulk form as to become more evenly balanced again, and to meet the luctuations in demand, Don Broomfield embarked on a hase of using demountable bodies with rigid four-wheelers. Blue Circle have long prided themselves on their valuation procedures whereby three or four years can be pent trying out a type or make of vehicle to see if it is perationally suitable. But a change in 1979 in the method f selling cement meant there was more incentive for a ustomer to buy 15- rather than 10-ton loads. Overnight, his marketing decision signalled the demise of the fleet's igid four-wheelers, and six-wheeled Leyland Bisons arrived pecifically to cater for this heavier chunk of traffic. owering these well liked Leylands were the TL11 and L12 ngines, a fitment also specified in the last 45 Routemen to e built, these coming into service during 1981. They were oined in 1983 by 75 Constructors, this batch being a mixture of six- and eight-wheelers. The eights, built by Scammell rather than Leyland, had Norde rubber suspension incorporated in the specification, saving a quarter of a ton each in unladen weight. These were the last rigids to be bought by Blue Circle, for the artic configuration came into favour with the company during the 1980s. Norman Gross was now in the post of Group Fleet Engineer and he sensed that the only way to meet the ever-changing surges between bag and bulk was to adopt articulation. The 20-ton load was still preferred by many customers and a large buying programme saw 200 two-axled Leyland Roadtrain tractive units come into service.

For bulk movements, Beddington built the first 30 non-tipping tank semi-trailers based on Metalair construction. This work was to end when Blue Circle Industries bought out the Metalair concern and the factory started doing the work direct for its new parent's transport arm. Changing circumstances meant that Beddington's role, which had lasted for 50 years, was close to an end. With a ready supply of trucks in a more competitive market-place, rebuilds carried out at Beddington, and all the other engineering depots, had long been a thing of the past. Another change was signalled in 1987 when Blue Circle offered discounts off the price of their cement for customers who arranged for their own collection. An option to use third-party haulage was thus available for a product that was now suffering from world-wide over-production. Both these factors were to contribute towards the shrinkage of the Blue Circle fleet.

In the early 1990s, the fleet size is only about a quarter of its 1,600 peak. Working out of 35 different locations throughout the UK, it is solidly based on Leyland Scammell 6x2 artic tractive units with Rolls-Royce 325 engines and Eaton Twin Splitter transmissions. All the vehicles are proudly emblazoned with the 70-year-old name of Blue Circle that still means just as much now as it has ever done in the field of cement production.

9: The Northern Clubs Federation Brewery Ltd

The British love of beer dates back as far as anyone can remember and the drink has been made, over the years, in every conceivable kind of brewery. Amongst them all, past and present, the Northern Clubs Federation Brewery Ltd, the 'Fed', has one of the most remarkable histories. Their brew, 'The Taste of Tyneside', is now well known throughout the country. From the modern, purpose-built brewery at Dunston, just off Newcastle's western by-pass, it is trunked as far afield as Penzance and Wick, and to countless places in between, by road vehicles mostly of British make. Like the beer, the 'Fed' fleet is well known in enthusiasts' circles.

It's not all long-distance work, of course. To some eyes, the ten AEC Mercurys still currently on the Federation books may seem rather old-fashioned, but they have paid for themselves time and time again and, on low daily mileage within the local Tyneside area, they still give very good service. The brewery and the drays alike have a reputation for longevity. But, whilst the days of the Mercurys are not being counted just yet, the fleet, like its brewing parent, has had to be flexible in adapting to the changing demands of the 1990s. These are exciting times for the Federation for, as you might deduce from the name, it is steeped in tradition and only in the last decade of its 70-year history has it begun to branch out, away from its original roots.

It seems difficult ever to visualize a situation where there would be a shortage of beer in this country but many ex-soldiers home from the Great War in 1919 encountered just such a state of affairs. What beer was available commanded a premium price, a totally unreasonable prospect for men who had fought for King and Country. But what they had perhaps learnt from the war was that right could prevail if enough people acted in co-operation. Social clubs had been founded all over the country where men could join together for relaxation and it was a group of these clubs in the Tyne Valley which were to combine to promote a unique federation that would combat this dearth of ale.

On May 24, 1919, representatives from Scotswood, Westerhope, Throckley, Ryton, Crawcrook, Greenside, Spen, Highfield and Mickley came to Prudhoe Social Club for what was to be a memorable occasion. In true Club style, a committee was formed to explore the possibility of acquiring a brewery that could produce drink for the clubs that were represented. That ultimate goal was to take some achieving, but the group of men soon realized that the buying power they could exert collectively augured well for a single approach direct to established brewers. The principle of buying from these people in bulk, then supplying to the individual clubs and thence to the membership at the wholesale prices was the foundation of the Federation of Clubs. To an assured supply was added the bonus of cheaper beer for club members at the end of the day.

This co-operative idea soon attracted many more clubs to join, but the enthusiasm for getting their own brewery nearly killed the Federation. It was suggested that the committee should bid £10,000 in 1921 to buy Smart's Brewery in Alnwick with a view to producing a Scotch-style beer. The proposal, backed specifically by support from the Northumberland members, where Alnwick was located, was passed and the sale agreed. The only problem was that no one had taken the time to inspect the brewery first and when they did, they found that the place was so dilapidated that it would never produce anything. Vigorous litigation reduced the original price to £7,750 but in essence it was money from the Federation of Clubs that went straight down the drain.

But their fortunes were to prove far better in Newcastle and, following the purchase of Deuchar's Brewery in Hedley Street for £4,300, the Northern Clubs produced the first Federation Brew in April 1921. Even deciding on the

pe of this first beer was done in a collective fashion by
stening to market research amongst the members. An
cidental effect of supplying the Clubs in the Federation
r subsequent sale at 6d (2½p) per pint was a costing level
at forced many private brewers to respond: for probably
e first time in their history, they had to reduce their
rices. As the gospel was spread round all manner of social
d workingmen's clubs, within a couple of years the
rtunes of the Federation were looking up and the quality
f brew that they produced was gaining widespread
ecognition. The albatross of Alnwick was a debt that was
on wiped clear and the Federation committee were able to
onate £1,000 to distressed miners during the 1926 General
trike.

The roots of the Federation were very much in the heavy
ndustry of the North-East, and these working men were
roving extremely thirsty. To cope with this continued
emand, another brewery, that of Buchanan's in Hanover
quare, was first leased and then bought in 1927 for
ederation use and it was from here that the 'Fed' really
egan to grow. By 1930 annual output had risen to 12,564
arrels and, if the Federation needed proof of the quality of

petrol-engined four-wheeled Albions were still in service at
the end of the 1950s, for the Federation made sure from the
earliest stage that they were certainly going to get a lifetime
of service out of each vehicle. The Albions did the
Federation well, although getting any more than about
5mpg wasn't usual. When loaded, they were pleasant and
stable vehicles to drive but when empty they were a bit of
a handful. Mel Heighway, now Traffic Manager at the
'Fed', recalls that when driving an empty Albion over the
multitude of cobbles in Newcastle you shimmied along like
a disjointed, waddling duck.

Mel came to the Federation in 1959, which was not long
after yet another extension to the brewery had been
completed. Its capacity was now recognized as 7,500 barrels
of beer plus 50,000 dozen bottles, and that was just in a
week. Lest you think this excessive, Mel recalls that some
clubs were getting deliveries of 30 hogsheads, twice a week.
When this is linked to supplying, at their peak, 1,000
different clubs, you begin to appreciate how busy the
Federation drays were.

To keep up with the demand, the committee decided to
buy an eight-wheeler, an AEC Mammoth Major, which

The petrol-engined Albion four-wheeler
was the Federation fleet stalwart right up
to the early 1960s. This Ian Wilkinson
photograph shows two model FT3s at the
Hanover Square brewery loading dock in
about 1948. The three-man crew are
handling 54-gallon hogsheads which tipped
the scales at about 7cwt a time. Jim
Wilkinson identifies one of the cabs of this
pair as having been made by the Co-
operative Wholesale Society when they had
a coachworks at Byker in Newcastle. These
lorries were rated for 5.2 tons of payload
and had a side-valve six-cylinder engine
which returned about 7mpg.

their products, this was given in 1931 when they swept the
board of medals at the prestigious annual Brewers'
Exhibition.

In 1933, the committee decided it was a good idea to start
purchasing their own transport vehicles, although it wasn't
until six years later that a garage was built to accommodate
them in what was then the new Orchard Street extension
that was opened on August 26, 1939. During the wartime
years, the Federation Brewery kept up full production as
beer wasn't deemed to be a luxury but more of a necessity
to hard-working men and women. Delivering the brew, the
Federation had opted for Albions, a marque they were to
stay with until the mid-1960s. In fact, some of the early

joined some AEC Monarch four-wheelers that were newer
companions to the petrol-engined Albions. The Mammoth
Major was the flagship of the fleet, which in the late 1950s
stood at about 30 strong. The big AEC's one obvious
drawback for the 'Fed' fitting staff was that it was far too
long: shoe-horning it into the garage for repairs was a work
of art. To make sure you got the eight-wheeler into the
garage, you had to drive it to a point where you bumped
into the end wall in front of you. You hadn't to hit the wall
too hard for, if you went through, it was an unstoppable
drop down to the Tyne quayside beyond! Once in this
position, the only way you could close the garage doors and
keep out the bleak northern weather as you worked on

As the Albions left, the Federation took the AEC Mercury as the standa workhorse and many are still runni today. Fleet number 9 was donated to t Historic Commercial Vehicle Socie North-East Branch, and is pictured on way to Sella Services where it was to stripped of its fixed tanks. These were combination of 90-gallon and 180-galle sizes and were discharged by pressu from on-board carbon dioxide cylinde Bobby Anderson was the last regular driv of this Mercury which was mostly used local Tyneside work. Opposite: amo drivers who have regularly worked in a out of Tyneside, some will no dou remember the Federation Marathor which seemed to be in a class of their ow as far as speed over the ground wa concerned. Jackie Guthrie was the regul driver of number 59 which was one of fi similar tractors, all with the TL12 engine

repairs was if you took off the door handles, giving an extra inch or so to clear the back of the AEC's body.

With the eight-wheeler once inside, it literally cut the garage in half. So to get from one side to the other – rather than have to crawl on all fours underneath – the Federation fitters built two sets of steps which were placed on either side of the AEC's body. This allowed you to walk up one side, across the platform body and down the other set of steps to reach the far side of the wagon and garage. Once the maintenance had been finished, there was a lengthy reverse up the street to a point where the AEC could be turned round. But these drawbacks apart, the sole Mammoth Major did the 'Fed' proud. It was also their first true long-distance wagon for, when the gospel had reached

Barrow-in-Furness, the big AEC used to run deliveries t that part of the North-West even though it was a two-day overnight job.

One vehicle which stayed very much closer to home wa a small Scammell Scarab three-wheeled mechanical hors which was coupled to a single-compartment tank semi trailer. Its sole job was to feed the bright beer room wit supplies to keep the bottling plant going and, as the cro flew, it just took beer from one side of the street to th other. The route the Scarab had to take entailed a trek o about 500 yards, and about 100 yards of this was in reverse Anyone who has tried this mode with the tight little arti will know it's not the easiest of tasks. The regular driver o the little Scammell, Tommy Burnett, was never very happ

The Federation used all the variants of the Leyland Boxer: fleet number 58 was rated at 12 tons gross. Four 16-ton Boxers were sent from Newcastle when the Penrith distribution depot was first set up. As well as carrying kegs and bottles, the vehicles had a dozen 14lb gas bottles in the side racking. The 698 engine was recalled as being rather 'soft', with leaking liner seals and piston troubles a regular occurrence.

Above right: bought specifically as a shunter from Tillotsons at Hull in about 1980, this 760-powered AEC Mandator was actually run on some distance work before being converted in-house for recovery duties. It carries a Harvey Frost hand-operated crane, and now has its original registration, VBT 626J, being taxed at the recovery rate. George Davies shares the photograph, the longest server in the garage with 23 years at the 'Fed' behind him.
Right: bought second-hand in about 1986, this 'B' type ERF had spent the first part of its life hauling eggs from a base in Cumbria. The Federation treat the Cummins-powered unit specifically as a spare motor, only sending it on trunk runs if the rest of the fleet is pushed. It spends most of its time running locally or, as when photographed in February 1991, taking trailers for test. Partially hidden behind the curtains are a set of old tanks filled with sand as test ballast.

in such a long back street so fitters like Mel Heighway, who had more practice than most just getting the artic out of the garage, were normally called in for this neck-wrenching manoeuvre.

The Federation had been obliged to buy this little tanker because they had been prevented from running a pipeline – even high in the air – from the main brewery across to the bottling area. The Scammell was kept in service until the bottling plant was moved back across to the source of supply, but it was another strange quirk of geography that was to be the biggest headache of the Federation. They hadn't really been concerned about it back in 1927 but in the 1950s and '60s, with member clubs screaming out for more and more produce, it turned out that further expansion was curtailed dramatically by an Ancient Monument. The city wall of Newcastle is a fine historical landmark but when this seven-foot-deep construction runs through the heart of your brewery, it takes some living with. In fact, the Federation had to live with the fact that members of the public were to be given access through the brewery just to read an inscribed plaque inserted in the

wall. They also had to accept that a member of the National Trust was almost a resident in the plant to ensure the wall wasn't inadvertently damaged.

These problems of internal logistics didn't prevent the Federation brews reaching further and further afield. In 1969, following representations by a group of northern MPs for a good northern brew to be sold in the Palace of Westminster, it was the Federation beer that went on sale in the Houses of Parliament at 2/3d (11p) per pint. Delivering that beverage was now in the hands of a fleet of AEC Mercury four-wheelers and Marshal six-wheelers. The sole Mammoth Major eight-legger had been a casualty of the newly introduced plating and testing legislation for, with no braking system fitted on the second steering axle, it couldn't meet the strict standard demanded. To conform with the rules, the vehicle was converted into a six-wheeler but what had been a pleasant wagon to drive changed to a monster with that second axle removed.

The committee had kept buying the AECs following good service given by their predecessors and it has long been a Federation doctrine to buy British for both their

The trunk wagons of the Federation fleet work a rota system so that the long-distance vehicles are sometimes seen on more mundane local work. Number 61 is pictured at the Dunston garage complex in the area set aside for incoming drays to deposit their assortment of empties. After checking and sorting, the kegs are reloaded and taken the short distance back to the main brewery for refilling. Raymond Bousefield is the regular driver of this Rolls-Royce 290-powered Roadtrain which was bought second-hand from the Manchester area.

truck and car fleet. In the early 1960s they tried the Commer TS3s which were ideal for a three-man crew but were found to be noisy and plain hard work to maintain and above all weren't expected to give the long life-span the AECs had proved capable of. The profile of those Ergomatic Mercurys was set to change as the Federation converted to tanker delivery. Against the trend to 5,000-gallon multi-compartment bulkers, the 'Fed' adopted 2½- and 5-barrel sizes of tank that were mounted in multiples on a flat-back Mercury. These fed into similar-sized containers at the points of discharge. Being of a manageable size, they also suited the changing social trend towards a far wider choice of drinks.

The 1960s had seen an unprecedented growth in demand for the products of the brewery as every form of sports, church and even Conservative club had taken advantage of the original Federation constitution. The transport fleet had long since outgrown its 1939 site, and in 1973 moved to its present base on Wellington Road, Dunston, very close to where a new brewery was to be built and officially opened on June 17, 1980. The 1970s also saw a big change in distribution as no longer could everyone be served from Newcastle. In 1976 a new distribution depot was set up in Torrington Avenue, Coventry which would look after supply to outlets in the southern part of England. Depots were also created at Castleford in West Yorkshire and at Penrith in Cumbria.

Feeding these far flung Federation points was to be the role of a trunking section in the transport fleet which has grown to a point where currently about a dozen artics are on the road every day. The first 32-tonner was headed up, naturally, by an AEC Mandator but this was one of the last to come out of Southall before the marque's demise. A quartet of Marathons followed and, with power provided by the TL12 engine, their pace across the ground is recalled as quite phenomenal. It is only quite recently that the last of the R- and S-registered Marathons have gone. Like the Rolls-Royce 265-powered Roadtrains that were to follow, plus the rest of the fleet, they were to adopt an entirely new livery. The new blue paint scheme, still in use, was actually prompted by the launch of the Federation's Medallion lager which had the same blue colour on the pump head. The Board decided that it was time for a change of image. Although the Federation had long prided itself on its 'Guaranteed Gravity' slogan, the social change in drinking

patterns meant that whilst 'Fed Special' may still have been supreme, it wasn't the only drink that was being supplied.

The opening of the new brewery at Dunston in 1980 also coincided with the beginning of the decline of all the major industries which historically had been the backbone of the North-East of England. The Federation had to reassess its strategy quickly in the face of a significant drop in beer drinking coupled to the changes in the social structure of the country generally. But rather than mourning the era passing, the 'Fed' has shown how it can prosper in the face of some wide new competition. In 1987 the Federation was to beat 143 entries from 63 breweries representing 31 countries when their LCL Pils Lager was voted 'The World's Best Bottled Lager' – and with no 'probably' about it! It's all the more remarkable when you learn that LCL (low carbohydrate lager) was first instigated when ex-Chairman Vic Dillon approached the brewers and asked if they could produce something better for diabetic people like himself to drink.

LCL is now just one of about 20 different brews that the Federation produces. Having gained such high repute both here and abroad in its trade, the 'Fed' is now involved in both a far wider range of products and a far wider range of services than those founding pioneers back in 1919 could ever have imagined. Opening their first public house, the 'Cutty Sark' in London, has been followed by four more and, along with the Hanover Wines chain of off-licences (which were later sold on), it heralded an entirely new era for this North-East concern.

Distribution Manager at the Federation is Rex Biggs who can undoubtedly be proud of 'The Taste of Tyneside' that his fleet carries even though it may sometimes have 'Tesco' or 'Littlewoods' written on the outside of the cans. A relocation of depots in 1989 saw a new site on Trafford Park in Manchester replace Castleford and Penrith as the Federation fleet adapted to the better links provided by the motorway network. The long-lived Mercurys that served the Federation in its first flowering may have lost some of their original fleetness of foot but, no matter what befalls the current hard-working line-up, one of the 1967 AECs is currently being preserved for posterity in the old Federation livery. It will be a fine reminder of the history of a concern which now sees an annual turnover around £60 million and is firmly established as part of a major industry where it is simply known as the 'Fed'.

Seen in about 1986 sporting a new paint job indicative of its recent arrival at Dunston, B773 ENL was bought second-hand through the local Seddon Atkinson dealer, Longfield Motors. This 301 has the Cummins 10-litre engine and Fuller nine-speed gearbox. It is fully loaded with 11-gallon kegs of Tyneside's best taste for delivery to the Coventry distribution depot. Above, right: after a big reorganization of distribution work, the Federation are opting for sleeper cabs on their trunk vehicles, reflecting the wide area they are now covering. Bought specifically to operate at the heavier weight band of 38 tonnes, this Scania 112 has Ray Newton as one of its regular drivers and joined the fleet on April 1, 1990. It is here loading full kegs out of the Dunston warehouse bound for either Coventry or Manchester. Below: coming new into service in November 1987 were a trio of Seddon Atkinson drop-frame four-wheelers, all of which are used out of the Dunston depot on dray delivery. Second man Sid Head is seen unloading at Throckley from the Laurence David bodywork, both the model of truck and the curtain sides being new ideas for the 'Fed' in this line of work. The vehicle has the Perkins Phaser engine which is reckoned to perform quite well, but the lack of steering lock on these four-wheelers has found its critics.

10: Richard Read (Transport) Ltd

Road haulage could well be described as one of our strangest service industries. It would be hard to exaggerate its importance, for without doubt it keeps the life blood of our country circulating. Yet, apart from one period of partial nationalization, it has thrived on sharp competition among men prepared to give their all – not, you might perhaps think, an atmosphere likely to ensure the all-important qualities of consistent service and long-term dependability. But, whilst it is true that haulage concerns have come and gone, there are nevertheless many operators whose long standing has given the industry the essential backbone of continuity that it needs.

That Richard Read (Transport) Ltd belongs in this category is not simply because the company's founder has spent more than 43 years in transport. He was influenced by his father, who began hauling in 1913, but more important is the fact that Richard Read, supported by his wife and family plus many long-serving members of staff, has provided a diversity of services with a degree of dedication to the task which may not be a monopoly of his company but is very much its trade mark. Clearly this approach springs from family characteristics, but it could also have something to do with geographical location. In western Gloucestershire, just as the name Dean is synonymous with the Forest, so Read is always mentioned in the same breath as transport.

It was to be the industries spawned by the Forest of Dean which were to lift Henry Read up the transport ladder, but that wasn't until the 1930s: originally, Richard's father set out moving what was very much a man-made product. The constituents of cement are naturally available, but it's hardly a rural pursuit and hauling 100 tons a day in 2cwt sacks from the Mitcheldean Cement Works to the local railway station for onward transport was plain hard work for the crew of three. Read used a steam traction engine which hauled three drawbar trailers and, rather like the men involved, it sweated bucketfuls and made a lot of noise getting through its daily tasks.

The Read steamer was quite famous in the area, its fame ensuring that, when engines were being requisitioned for the First World War, it was one of the earliest to be commandeered. Henry Read went with his faithful power-house across to France but, whilst he was able to come back to Longhope in 1918, the steamer ended its days in those war-torn years. During the 1920s and '30s, Read built up his transport fleet to about seven vehicles. Ex-army Peerless chain-drives afforded extra traction in the heart of the Forest but Studebaker, Leyland and Albion were also used to haul coal and stone from the Forest's collieries and quarries normally, again, to the local railhead.

Come 1940, the Read business was hit once again by the war effort as vehicles and drivers were commandeered so, deciding to call it a day, Henry passed the remnants of the concern to George, one of his eight sons, who had already set himself up in the haulage business. Younger brother Richard had stretched the age limits marginally so that he had been driving one of his father's Albion KL127 coal wagons in the Forest at the age of 16, but most of the wartime period saw him in the Royal Navy working on a minesweeper, mainly off the African coast.

Back in Gloucestershire in 1946, Richard Read was to make two decisions that were to affect him for the rest of his life. The first one was to marry Amelia and the second one saw him leave the driving job he had with his brother's firm. He had the urge to be his own boss and, to build up a stake to launch him into transport, young Richard went in for sinking wells. No, it wasn't oil he was after but simply water at a time when there was a house-building boom in the area. No sophisticated drilling rig to hand, all that Read used was a spade and the bend in his back.

This hard work honed him up for things to come. The £350 he pulled together was handed over to Charlie

Morgan at Pengam in exchange for an ex-army petrol-engined Albion six-wheeler. Its original tilt body was discarded in place of a conventional dropside one and both vehicle and its new owner-driver were to be severely hammered in their first line of work. In 1947, construction was starting on the Gloucester ring road and as it was built on a bed of clay, copious amounts of stone were needed to give the road some solid foundations. In his first month of operation, Richard Read recalled, he handled 1,350 tons of the stuff. Not hauled but handled, for the figure he remembers is having to handball 625 tons of stone out of the quarry on to the back of the Albion; then once at the delivery point he had to shovel and manhandle the same 625 tons off again.

That first four weeks in business taught him a lot, and it also won him a contract to move another 30,000 tons for the Severn Water Authority. But Read knew his efficiency had to improve so he went out and bought the scrap remnants of an ex-County Council Morris Commercial. Whilst the vehicle was of no interest to the young entrepreneur, what he was after was its tipping body mechanism which he shoe-horned into his trusty Albion. The old Albion did Read well. It gave of its best as it rattled down the beat between the site on the banks of the River Severn and the Forest quarries. With upswept induction into the petrol engine's carburettor, the Albion seemed to perform better when there was a slight dew on the ground. Red hot sunny days were not for this vehicle as vapour lock would simply slow it down.

Read's fortunes were set to improve. He bought a little Dodge four-wheeler tipper and, as the Albion simply wore itself out, he invested his earnings in KFH 8, a brand-new Bedford four-wheeler. But vehicles were of little use at that time without a suitable carrier's licence and, although you could always try and apply for a new licence, the hassle resulting from the level of objections raised meant it was easier, if more expensive, to just go out and buy whatever was up for sale.

A Dodge on an 'A' licence was bought from Townsend of Blakemoor Farm, but it was buying the four vehicles of Billy Hoare from Coleford that really launched Read into fleet haulage. Administering operations was the role that Amelia Read took over, a post that she is still involved with right up to the present day. The Read base was a cottage at Little London and, when not on the move, the vehicles were parked up on a farm at Royal Spring. The second brand-new vehicle on fleet was a Seddon dropside four-wheeler with a Perkins P6 engine bought by Read from dealer Wilson Scott at Gloucester. Reasonably fond memories of this vehicle contrast to those of a second-hand Thornycroft Sturdy Star whose history of valve bounce and subsequent valve spring breakage proved a bit of a nightmare.

Strangely, the big nationalization programme of 1949 was not a nightmare for Reads. They were running about seven vehicles then and the subsequent curtailment of activities to a pre-set radius of 25 miles from Longhope Post Office was something, initially at least, they could live with. Carrying

traffic beyond that circle was only allowed if you were granted a permit for the load from the Lord and Masters of the Road Haulage Executive. Gloucester permits were issued from a large house on Escort Road roundabout but getting something from permit-man Tom Thomas was real blood-out-of-stone work. If British Road Services had one of their own vehicles standing, then a permit was refused on the grounds that they would do the work instead. Although you could always take a chance and run without the permit, Read devised a different line that may have been cheeky but was definitely legal.

One aspect of traffic that wasn't part of the nationalized programme was own-account work: in other words, you

Although the all-encompassing nationalization programme that swathed through the road-transport industry in the late 1940s made people do some strange things, this photograph wasn't specifically meant to illustrate Richard Read's feelings on the subject. The scene is the depot in Mitcheldean of his brother, George Read, which in 1949 had just fallen under the BRS banner, and Richard was there for a local carnival.

TDG 689 was Richard Read's first brand new ERF and his first taste of articulation. The tandem-axle semi-trailer was of Scammell manufacture, bought second-hand from Rush Green Motors at Hitchin. The vehicle had a Gardner 6LW engine, first went into service in 1957, with Eddie Overthrow as regular driver, and went on to be used by the haulier for almost 20 years. A more modern cab was fitted after the original had been damaged when a loading crane jib snapped and fell on the roof.

could transport your own goods without interference from the RHE. Richard Read developed this line of latitude by going into the business of buying and selling the loads he carried. Obviously he could only do it with people he knew and trusted but legally, once he had bought, say, a load of timber in the Forest, he was quite entitled to take it to Scotland if he wished and he could there sell it on to a waiting customer. The difference in buying and selling prices may only have incorporated his transporting costs but at least it was a taste of true long-distance work.

This ruse was a good one, but getting back into proper licensed transport in the period of denationalization was certainly a relief. 1953 saw various lots of BRS vehicles being offered for sale by tender and the first acquisition by the 28-year-old Read was the former fleet of haulier Morgan & Friend from Hereford. Four Seddons and two Proctors were the four-wheeled dropsiders he bought and at £1,100 a time it showed how good a price an open 'A' licence could fetch. Four Maudslays from the BRS Pontypool depot were to follow, and by now Read was looking for a more suitable operating base.

An 11-acre site was bought at Longhope and, although

These sister 6LW-powered eight-wheelers with 18ft wheelbase came into service new during February 1958. Their first work was hauling paper pulp from Sudbrook Pulp Mills to Dartford in Kent. Productivity was increased by hauling drawbar trailers, the early crews including driver Harold Bullock and trailer mates Keith Lord and Owen Price. Even running as 'wagon and drag' outfits at close to 32 tons gross, the ERFs were only fitted with Girling hydraulic brakes assisted by an air servo. But the spec did include the chrome front bumper, polished trim strips round the wheelarches, twin windscreen wipers and the luxury of twin demisters. UDF 464 had chassis number 8544 and was priced net ex-works at £4,333 13s 11d.

During 1959, Dennis Foden approached Richard Read to take a long-term demonstrator on trial, 347 GLG being the first ERF to have the Perkins 6.354 engine. The four-wheeler was to do 300,000 trouble-free miles with that engine before it was replaced with a similar Perkins unit, the transplant being performed so that ERF could examine the innards. This is the Longhope base in April 1961: the filling station was to be a casualty of the village by-pass construction which took a slice off the front of the Read property.

he needed a permit to build his bungalow home, the size and location were ideal for the job. It didn't prove too ideal for nearby householders, though, for the Read transport empire was about to explode. Getting planning permission to move the wagons yet again was always going to be difficult but once the local council indicated that they would help in cutting the red tape, moving the fleet out to the current site of operations on the edge of Longhope was a choice they leapt at.

By the time of this move, in 1957, the Read operations had been rapidly diversifying away from their earlier staple traffic. A contract hauling the tiles from H. & G. Thynne of Hereford was won and took their glazed products all over the country. Albion Chieftain and Dodge four-wheelers were the main company work-horses at the time but for the heavy boxed tiles Maudslay 'Chinese Sixes', ex-Usher brewery, were more suitable, as was the first brand-new

Atkinson eight-wheeler. MVJ 681 arrived on June 1, 1955, and was entrusted to long-serving driver Ken Hardwick. The Gardner engine, David Brown gearbox and Kirkstall bogie was a specification which Read took to, and more Atkinsons would have been bought were it not for the persistence of Harold Sansum. Previously having worked with Sentinels at Shrewsbury, Sansum was Sales Manager at ERF and it was his hard pitch that convinced Read to take his favoured specification but to have it in an ERF chassis. Read agreed, and this first ERF, TDG 689, was also the company's first artic tractor unit. A big investment on the tractor was compensated for by buying a second-hand trailer from Rush Green Motors, which, when shot blasted and refurbished, was to give Reads excellent value for money.

Read might just have continued to use ERFs in his fleet but, as it turned out, it developed into something more than

Fitted with the more usual Gardner 4LW engine, this four-wheeled ERF had an Eaton two-speed axle driven through a David Brown gearbox. The Edbro tipping gear supports a Nash & Morgan body, its dropside construction topped out with 'greedy boards' allowing a whole variety of cargoes to be carried on the long wheelbase. Coal and sugar beet were some of its typical loads, and it also hauled a lot of flint as back-loads from Dartford.

This CVRTC photograph shows a rare sight in the Read fleet, the second-hand Leyland Octopus eight-wheeled tipper dating from 1961. As the high 'greedy boards' suggest, its staple traffic was coke from the South Wales work, hauled on a regular beat across to a smelting foundry at Enfield. Ron Lewis recalls that the only other Leyland run at that time was a Beaver tractor unit coupled to a BTC four-in-line semi-trailer. Running pulp out of Sudbrook down to the tissue factories in South Wales meant traversing the streets of Cardiff and Bridgend, and the Beaver's heavy clutch made it very hard work.

that. The abrupt bankruptcy of the tile maker Thynne, a good customer of Read's, was totally unforeseen. Three brand-new eight-wheelers had just been ordered on the strength of their traffic. When Read let ERF know the circumstances and said that he could only afford to pay for one of the eight-leggers, the Cheshire manufacturer told him simply to pay for the other two when he could. Read had always done business before by paying outright as he went along, so this helpful attitude on the part of ERF made him determined not to let them down.

Just 13 months later, work out of Whitehead Steel at Newport and paper-pulp traffic from Wiggins Teape at Sudbrook had ensured that the two eight-wheelers and their drawbar trailers were paid for. Read enquired how much interest he owed on this deferred settlement but Dennis Foden's response, waiving any extra payment, came with the message of 'Keep on buying ERFs, that's all we would like'. Read went better than that: his enthusiasm for the marque prompted sales of a 6LW tractor unit to his cousin in Hereford, a four-wheeler to a local potato merchant and a 4LW unit to H.R. Robinsons of Hereford. The orders had gone direct to Sun Works so Read won himself the salesman's commission and also a request to be the ERF distributor for Gloucestershire and Herefordshire.

Richard Read (Commercials) Ltd was set up in 1960 as an entirely different business from Richard Read (Transport) Ltd which was incorporated on March 21, 1963, albeit both concerns were based at the same Longhope site. Naturally all new vehicles taken into the transport fleet after that were to be ERF. Probably the last exception was 7733 AD, a lightweight Albion Reiver. Ron Lewis was given this new vehicle in 1960, having come to Reads with the bought-out fleet of vehicles and licences from J.T. Phillips of Gorsley. Ron recalls that this Albion probably paid for its entire keep during the winter of 1963 when it was the only Read vehicle which could climb out of Longhope on the treacherous snow-covered roads. On the

run down the A40 to London with paper pulp, the bleak conditions over the Cotswolds led the police to stop all lorries at the Windrush Cafe. But when the drivers had eaten the Cafe out of all its foodstocks, the Reiver's surefootedness made it one of the few vehicles that could carry on.

The Albion was to be Lewis's last taste of a rigid, as a series of ERF artics were lined up for him. His first 'A'-series had a Gardner 150 engine and a rather ponderous top-speed capability of 42mph – and that was on the overrun. Its replacement, another 'A'-series, was fitted with a Cummins 180 engine which had a lot more go than the 6LX but it was its innovative Jacobs engine brake that was the real head-turner. Running downhill on the 'Jake Brake' gave a lot of peace of mind for the driver but created a terrific noise from the exhaust. West Wycombe police regularly stopped Ron to complain about the racket he was making until Jacobs devised a quieter system for their back-pressure device.

During the 1960s, the Read fleet grew to an all-time high of 87, all of which were under the day-to-day control of Amelia Read. Selling ERFs wasn't the only other business of Reads as they also became agents for BTC trailers, manufactured at Trafford Park, Manchester. BTC were famous for their four-in-lines, which, although very light, were a driver's nightmare when you had a blow-out on one of the inner tyres. Reads also sold Highway trailers which were of conventional tandem-axle design, the Southampton manufacturer using a flying elephant as its logo. The only thing that Reads had to stop doing during the late 1960s was selling fuel: their petrol pumps were a casualty to the newly built Longhope by-pass which took a large slice from the frontage of their six-acre site.

An entirely new venture in 1974 was Read's involvement in Vijore, the name being a compilation from Vick, Jones and Read. Along with Eric Vick and Tony Jones, Reads joined in a £7-million contract moving a diverse range of

eads were also agents for Dodge sales and rvice, and 2594 DG was one of five milar tractor units they ran, Richard ead himself being pictured here behind e wheel. The Dodge had a Perkins 6.354 ngine and the BTC four-in-line semi-ailer carries bodywork by Atkinsons of litheroe. The vehicle, seen here at onghope in 1963, was normally used for oal delivery around Gloucestershire chools.

agricultural equipment overland to Baghdad. This job was to last for close on two years. Then, although more Continental work was still being generated, Read decided to leave Vick and Jones to it. A changing pattern of seeking groupage meant this Iraq service was never as smooth to control or organize, making Read unhappy about continued involvement.

This decision gives some indication of Read's philosophical attitude in his approach to his chosen business of transport. A resolve never to be unnecessarily dictated to was well illustrated when he felt the unions were making unreasonable demands in the late 1970s. Richard Reads weren't the only haulier to suffer a drivers' strike to further a pay claim but Read's answer was simply to have three-quarters of his fleet auctioned off. As well as raising very good prices the Read sales prompted a fair bit of media attention, although that interest paled into insignificance when compared to the publicity experienced in 1984.

One line of work that Reads have done for many years, and still continue to do, is hauling coke from Port Talbot Steelworks to Commonwealth Smelting at Avonmouth. In March 1984, Reads had 12 vehicles on this traffic, all of

As a notable dealership, Reads found themselves participating in many of the big shows in the area, this particular shot being taken at the 1961 Three Counties Show in Malvern. Richard Read, left, stands with his wife Amelia, and Norman Upton, who joined the company as sales manager that year. The ERF 2LV, painted white, has another Atkinson-built body and was also used to deliver coal to Gloucestershire schools before switching to potatoes for Smiths Crisps.

The Reads have long been active on t[...] vintage rally scene and their 19[...] Thornycroft is quite a head-turner. Boug[...] in about 1970 from Briggs timber yard[...] Gloucester, it underwent a major rebui[...] to bring it up to its current better-tha[...] new condition. The four-cylinder petr[...] engine has four priming cups which a[...] filled with fuel for starting: hand-cranki[...] it then usually fires one cylinder and t[...] others follow in sympathy.

which suffered much attention from the massive pickets of striking coal miners. His vehicles were smashed up, his drivers were threatened and, although Read had meetings with the miners' representatives, the strikers said that they had no intention of stopping their actions until Read's vehicles stopped moving the coke. At the time this was a scenario which was being repeated all over the country and most hauliers, prompted by guidance from their customers, simply had vehicles parked up as they waited things out. No one knew the strike was to last for a year, but Richard Read decided on a more positive course of action.

Accompanied by his nephew George Read, who was also running wagons on the coke job, Read made application at the High Court in London for an injunction to prevent this abuse of his vehicles and staff. It wasn't surprising that o[...] April 11, 1984, Judge Sir Douglas Frank QC granted th[...] injunction under the provisions of the Employmen[...] Protection Act against the South Wales Area of the Nationa[...] Union of Mineworkers. But what had been surprising wa[...] how the Reads – described in the Press as rather small fish[...] – took on the might of the NUM whilst bigge[...] organizations just sat back and did nothing.

In response to the injunction, the NUM did nothing and[...] picketing of the Reads continued. On July 31, 1984, the[...] Reads went back to court and, for failing to comply with the[...] injunction, the NUM were fined a total of £50,000. This[...] wasn't to be the end of the story for, although the NUM[...] eventually stopped their picketing, Reads found themselves[...]

Built originally as a heavy-duty tractive unit for export, this ERF was bought new by Reads in 1980 to be converted into a recovery vehicle. With a Cummins 290 engine driving through a Fuller 9509B gearbox, it has a spread of performance ranging from a 70mph top speed to the ability to crawl like a snail. Standing in at a kerbside weight of 22 tons in normal running order, the 6x4 chassis supports wrecking gear which started life on a military Leyland Martian. Following changes in trade-plate law, the ERF is now registered Q399 FDD.

Its looks belying its double-figure age, LAW 971P is seen at the Longhope depot in July 1987 during the second phase of its working life. The vehicle was sold new by Reads to B & J Davies and run with a non-tipping body and crane on timber haulage. It was subsequently part exchanged for another new truck supplied by Reads who then decided to keep it, fit a tipper body and use it in their own fleet. At the time of writing, the Cummins 240-powered ERF has been sold again and is still at work in the Ross area.

The A4136 Gloucester to Monmouth road offers the traveller both magnificent countryside and this most impressive view of the Read depot. True, Richard Read junior only lines the fleet up like this on bank holidays, but the resultant spectacle is a marvellous advert for both Reads and ERF.

being blacked by the Transport Union as a sign of support for the NUM.

More court appearances followed and even now, seven years on, the bitter taste of the whole episode hasn't been forgotten. As to why he did it, a quote from Richard Read at the time may give some indication: 'We thought the whole thing through and considered all the consequences. We take our own decisions, we work for ourselves and we take counsel from nobody.'

It is apparent that Reads work extremely hard for themselves. In 1988 the Commercial side of affairs, which has Norman Upton as Sales Manager, won the coveted ERF Dealer of the Year award. Norman joined Reads in 1961, and along with other long-servers John Cox, Lawrence Taylor, Ron Lewis and Miriam Knight, he shares in 150 years of company service. In 1990, Richard Read qualified for his pensioner's bus pass and whilst he and wife Amelia are supposed to be enjoying more of an overseeing role these days, the Read attitude makes this very much a matter of active participation! With son Richard, daughter-in-law Kay and daughter Brenda in the business, the Read contribution to haulage shows no sign of diminishing.

11: Gilbraith Tankers Ltd

Movements of liquids, powders and gas in bulk occupy a big slice of UK road haulage equipment. Whilst this side of the industry sometimes seems to be dominated by the larger conglomerates, there are smaller independent forces at work here too, and one such is Gilbraith Tankers Ltd who have been busy running road tankers for more than 50 years. The fleet is now nearly 60 vehicles, and the immaculate Leyland Roadtrain five-axled 38-tonne chemical tankers are a distinctive sight throughout the motorway network. With bases including Warrington, Fleetwood, Hull and Carlisle, it is in the north of England that Gilbraith are particularly strong. Their head office, very much the heart of the operation, is at Atlas Works in the Clayton-le-Moors area of Accrington.

If you go to this part of north-east Lancashire, you just cannot avoid seeing the name Gilbraith. Many people in the area will have bought their private transport through Gilbraith Cars Ltd, while the haulage buyer is very likely to have had some dealings with Gilbraith Commercials Ltd. In its time, Gilbraith Transport Ltd ran over 120 wagons: that facet of the organization has since been consolidated, but Gilbraith Tankers Ltd remains distinct and thriving.

The first meeting of this limited company didn't take place until October 1, 1956. It was held at the Greyhound Garage, a place which is the cornerstone of the Gilbraith story. Back in 1920, Henry Gilbraith had sunk all £500 of his savings into buying the garage on the corner of Whalley Road and Whinney Hill in the Altham area of Accrington. To many people, this seemed a risky venture for Gilbraith who had served his apprenticeship with Broad Oak Printworks Ltd and was then employed as an engineer at the Moorlands Infirmary. In 1920 the popular use of the motor car was very much in its infancy – petrol was delivered to the garage in two-gallon cans by means of a horse and cart. Whilst fuel sales weren't going to make Henry a rich man, it was to be his engineering flair which

kept him busy, with contracted work in this line being obtained both at the local hospital and the brickworks.

An entirely different project was attempted in 1924 when an old charabanc was bought and converted in-house from passenger to goods-carrying use. This diversity of interests augured well for Gilbraith. Whilst many suffered during this period of recession, he expanded his haulage work and even had a small showroom built on to the garage site at Altham. In 1933, with the creation of the stifling carriers' licence system, Gilbraiths were issued with four 'A' licences under 'Grandfather's rights', this being the number of vehicles then in use. Growth was curtailed until Gilbraiths took over another haulage concern, and by 1940 the transport side of the business involved 12 vehicles. Although in essence it was a general haulage operation, the interesting point for this chapter was that one of those dozen was a four-wheeled rigid tanker. No great aspiration to specialize in bulk liquids had led to this acquisition, simply a requirement from a customer to move tar and heavy oil.

The purchase of Thomas Gilmartin Ltd in 1948 meant that when nationalization came to Accrington in 1949, Gilbraiths had about 30 vehicles in the fleet. Although only a couple of tankers were exempt from compulsory purchase, Gilbraiths adopted the simple ruse of selling some of their fleet to the Accrington Brick & Tile Company and then continuing to organize their operation. Obtaining permits for other vehicles to run up to a 60-mile radius on bagged and drummed chemical work meant in essence that Gilbraiths escaped total absorption into British Road Services.

Once the political decision was made to de-stock the BRS fleet, Gilbraith naturally started to make their bids and it was to be in the 1950s when the whole organization took off. Fleet size accelerated up to the 120 mark, with bases being opened at Liverpool, Scunthorpe and Leeds as well as

This Octopus, which dates from 1957, illustrates the new Gilbraith Tankers name but still carries a fleet number applicable to the old-established H. Gilbraith organization. Here unloading oil from Shell into Padiham power station, the Leyland is fitted with a tank constructed by Burnley Boilers.

Accrington. A chain of seven garages were now selling fuel at a rate of a million gallons per year. In contrast, the tanker side of affairs was rather modest. Allan Woods, who is currently Fleet Engineer at Blackburn Road, came to Gilbraiths in 1952 and his first memories of tank vehicles centre on a sole prewar Leyland four-wheeler, probably a Badger, fitted with the six-cylinder petrol engine. This was run predominantly on local work between Church and Altham until 1956 when the chassis was scrapped and the tank transferred on to a second-hand but gleaming Leyland Comet 300 flat that had done little work around the cotton mills near Burnley.

During the 1950s and even into the early '60s, Gilbraith's policy on vehicle selection was one of running whatever they could get their hands on. Indicative of this mixture is that vehicles like a Maudslay 'Chinese Six' rigid, a Thornycroft three-axled artic with Meadows engine and a trio of AEC six-wheelers were used for bulk liquid haulage. The latter were all ex-BRS Mammoth Majors, Gilbraith fitting them with converted tanks that had originally been made for storage purposes only. Against the background of this mix-and-make-do policy, it was something of a big day in 1955 when the first brand-new eight-wheeler came, with a purpose-built Butterfield tank fitted to the 24-ton (gross) chassis. Painted in finest transport red and adorned with gold lettering, 'H. Gilbraith Ltd', the Leyland Octopus VTB 504 seemed the epitome of its kind, but day two in its life was one that many people will never forget.

In the mid-1950s, although tankers were starting to become a more regular sight, they were still not common. Young Allan Woods was aware of most of them in the Accrington area but that day he saw one which really caught the eye. The main thing about it was its colour, a deep shining black. It was only when it got much closer and he was able to read the registration that he realized it was the pride and joy of Gilbraith's, the brand-new Leyland. An unfortunate accident spilling black oil during loading meant the cab was covered in a slow-drying black skin. It may have been a good idea to prevent rusting, but it wasn't an option that the company followed up!

Although they were still running tankers at only a fairly modest level, the explosion of Gilbraiths' affairs necessitated a rescheduling of the business. The creation of a separate company, Gilbraith Tankers Ltd, was one decision reached in 1956. Owing to uncertainty about how this mode of transport would develop, ownership of the new company was to be equally shared between Gilbraiths and Tar Residuals Ltd, their main customer for this class of vehicle. John and Philip Gilbraith, sons of Henry, took over the helm of this concern along with their other businesses. Reading the minutes of that first meeting in October 1956 gives some indication of what a low-key affair it was in the early stages. A question was raised whether an old AEC, JF 9264, should be repaired but that decision was put off until the next meeting. Consideration was also given as to whether they should order their fifth new tanker in the

Sharing the same cab as its Leyland eight-wheel counterpart, the Albion Caledonian never generated the same level of popularity as the evergreen Octopus. Number 3 was one of two of these wagons run by Gilbraith and had a six-compartment Yewco tank. This Albion had its own specially designed rear axle with an aluminium sump. One of these sumps was holed in a freak accident when a stone was thrown up at it. Len Fenning, the fitter on call at the time, knew he was in for a lengthy roadside repair and took his wife and family with him to make a day of it.

following year but even that was deferred.

What tankers did come were to be fitted on new chassis, with a mixture of Leyland Octopus rigids and maximum-weight Scammell artics being favoured. A couple of Albion Caledonian eight-wheelers were also bought and, although they shared the same engine and cab as their Leyland Octopus stablemate, they had a couple of subtle differences. One was an air-over-hydraulic braking system rather than direct air, but the real driver's delight was power-assisted steering, quite a luxury in 1958 – although engineer Woods recalls that the system's pump could be a right swine to work on.

In 1960, company founder Henry Gilbraith died, leaving his sons John and Philip a considerable legacy. The garage and car sales part of the empire was a huge business in itself, and among the road haulage fleet, now in three figures, there were more than 60 tippers kept very busy. The tanker side of the business had been more modest in expansion but by 1962 there were 27 vehicles on the books, ranging in capacity between 1,000 and 4,000 gallons. Stainless and mild steel tanks were used, fitted with pump or compressor discharge equipment. The main cargoes were still tar and the heavier liquids like fuel oil, bitumen, creosote and naphthalene. Heavyweight chassis in use included eight-wheeler Leylands like 533 WTD, then a fairly new Octopus.

With another big tanker, 557 TTB, Gilbraiths demonstrated their ability to haul other, non-liquid products. That registration was carried by a 6x4 Albion Reiver which ran on contract for Ribble Cement. It was one of three similar vehicles with Bonallock Pneumajector bodywork, its pressure discharge equipment being able to blow the cement to storage points up to 120ft high.

Whilst the late 1950s had been the boom time for tippers, the 1960s saw tanker operations undergo continued expansion. It was soon realized that this one-time infant of the Gilbraith family was overdue to leave home, and in June 1967 the company acquired their current HQ at Atlas Works. Geographically, the move to the old Taywil foundry site didn't involve any great distance but it did give Tankers the space to create their own identity.

Heading up affairs was to be W.K. (Ken) Birchall, who stayed as Managing Director until his retirement in 1984. His rise to become Chairman of the Road Haulage Association Tanker Functional Committee gives some indication of the stature of Gilbraiths in this specialized field. But the company now found itself under slightly different ownership. In 1965 Simon Engineering had taken over the 50% holding previously in the hands of Tar Residuals Ltd, though this meant little change in day-to-day operations as the fleet grew steadily.

In 1969, the current Operations Manager David Eatough came to the company and at that time, he recalls, they were running about 60 vehicles. About half of them were carrying tar-type products, a lot of work being done for Lancashire Tar Distillers, but the other half of the work involved the growing business of moving a wide range of chemicals in bulk. Even at this stage a number of tankers were based away from Accrington, and this wasn't without the odd local problem. Andy Young was one of the

This scene at Atlas Garage is not one that could be repeated today because the area occupied by the council offices has since disappeared under the new M65 motorway. The Leyland Comet seen here was a five-compartment four-wheeler used for local deliveries of derv and paraffin. The Scammell Pioneer was an ex-military breakdown vehicle, kept by Gilbraiths until 1985.

Number 171 was one of a quartet of Trunker IIs run by Gilbraiths, two of which had the semi-automatic gearbox whilst the other pair had the AEC six-speed box. It is seen coupled to a gas tank that was operated on a dedicated contract for ICI over a two-year period.

Liverpudlians who worked his Albion Caledonian on paraffin traffic out of the Dingle refinery on the Mersey. Such was his passion, however, for the 'Reds' football team, that if ever he was given the job to deliver near the Everton stadium then he would refuse point blank!

Vincent Kennedy was an Accrington driver from that period with a reputation for being extremely cantankerous, perhaps because he had undergone a hard upbringing. His first job when he left school had been as a driver's mate on a coal wagon and his main task, after the lorry had been loaded, was to sit on the back and fight people off who were trying to steal the coal. The tough side of the Kennedy nature was revealed after an accident which took place when he was unloading his tanker inside private premises at Newcastle. The coming together involved a railway engine and, although the Leyland wasn't badly hurt, the damage included the cab getting knocked off. Unperturbed, Kennedy secured a crude seat on to the exposed chassis and with no more ado drove back to the depot from the North-East. Almost frozen to the woodwork, the only thing he said on his arrival at Accrington was 'I want a pair of gloves'.

The Gilbraith tanker men often had a hard life. The tar and bitumen class of traffic was a particularly difficult product to handle as it had to be loaded boiling hot and then delivered, in the insulated tanks that Gilbraiths used, fairly quickly. This scheduling meant loading times could be anything from 12 midnight to 2am. Subsequent deliveries as far south as North Wales and Staffordshire were again timed, and if the tar was for a busy road building scheme, the nightmare of a breakdown was one that

Gilbraiths, with the solidifying product they were carrying, couldn't bear to think about.

As tools of the trade, the company favoured the Scammell Highwayman, and about 30 of these were taken into service. A dogged machine it may have been but it wasn't exactly a driver's favourite. Most Scammell men used cotton wool ear-plugs but even so, at the end of the day, with the plugs discarded, it still took about an hour before the effects of the bonneted Scammell died down enough to allow them to listen to the television.

The Commercials side of Gilbraiths had become a Leyland distributor for northern Lancashire in 1966, so naturally Leyland chassis began to be favoured for the whole group. One exception to this rule involved an urgent order for six new eight-wheelers when Leyland were only able to come up with four of them. Two ERFs were taken to meet the shortfall and their specification included disc brakes on the front axles. This entirely new concept in braking was quickly under the microscope as, on the first day out, one of the new ERFs ran straight into the back of the other one. No fault with the brakes however, it was thick fog which caused this unintended coming together.

There was no stopping the Gilbraith tanker expansion. The Atlas Works were deemed to be the finest of their kind, and the £30,000 investment included greasing, lubrication and inspection bays. Having a central traffic office with a direct link to the Fleet Engineer's office made for close operational liaison and the facilities on site also included both internal and external tank washes.

What was to stop the management in their tracks,

One-time foreman Stan Waddington was photographed at the wheel of his latest Scammell Handyman on August 11, 1972. Gilbraiths were to run a score of these four-wheeled tractive units, some with the Rolls-Royce 220 engine, the others with the Leyland 680 version. The phenol tank was built by Butterfield, its single-compartment double-cone or 'banana' design giving central discharge. Stan, still with the company, started his driving days with BRS.

BBV 254R was brand-new and just about to start work when this photograph was taken on August 16, 1976. Di Davies, still with Gilbraiths, is in the cab. The company ran a number of Buffalos with the 510 engine, nine-speed Fuller transmission and Maudslay back axle. These Leylands were good when running well but had an awful habit of breaking down with dropped valves. The mild-steel Universal tank is kitted up for full roll-over protection in recognition of the hazardous nature of the EDC product it was normally going to carry.

however, was a visit to the premises by Lancashire County Council in 1971. The bombshell they dropped was that plans for the newly proposed M65 meant that the Atlas Works would be completely wiped out under six lanes of tarmac. Although the path of the motorway was still at an early planning stage, Gilbraiths decided to take the threat of compulsory closure seriously and reassess their long-term future plans. Whilst historically Accrington was the Gilbraith heartland, changes in traffic flow meant some vehicles were running further afield to collect their loads. Dead mileage had been cut by basing about ten vehicles at Heysham and a further six at Fleetwood. Traditional

sources of bulk liquids like nearby Church were drying up so it was decided to make a complete break and head south, 40 miles closer to the Merseyside chemical belt.

The depot at Warrington, closely adjacent to both the M6 and the M62 motorways was soon established, although plans were sent awry again when Lancashire County Council came back for another visit about 1976. Gilbraiths were informed that the sweep of the motorway had been replanned after a public enquiry so now their depot would not be compulsorily acquired as only about a quarter would be sliced off for the new road. Gilbraiths had to rethink their tanker strategy once more, but the conscious decision run with two widely spread main operating centres was serve them well as the future unfolded. The steady cline in tar-like traffic coincided with a boom in emicals. Long before legislation had really woken up to e requirements of this hazardous traffic, Gilbraiths were ready enforcing their own very high standards of practice. 1973, together with the Safety Department of ICI uncorn, they assisted in creating a week-long course in river training which is the backbone of the present-day azchem training requirements. Gilbraiths too had long nce been clearly identifying their hazardous products so

the step to the then-optional Hazchem labelling was one that they totally supported.

The vehicles that were being adorned with the new orange labels were also on the change. Whilst the bonneted Highwaymen were at last going, Scammells were still favoured very strongly, with new Handymen IIs and a quartet of Trunker IIs coming. Gilbraiths did run a sole Scammell Handyman I artic and this was given first to Sam Phillips to try out. Being both a Scouser and an ex-paratrooper, Sam always tried to create a big tough image for himself but even he felt the steering on this new

eaving the premises of chemical anufacturer William Blythe at Church, river Russell Taylor is having his cumentation checked by the security an, another Taylor. Gilbraiths got good rvice from their TL12-powered arathons – gasket problems apart. Some etails of number 127's specification, cluding the Spicer gearbox, made it very milar to the soon-to-arrive Roadtrain nge. The Universal single-compartment nk normally carried a particularly heavy roduct and thus had a capacity of only 000 gallons.

ersatile: the SP prefix to the trailer fleet umber indicates a specially constructed nker used for very special traffic. Leyland umber 182 heads up an outfit that carries full-weight load of EDC in its first and ird compartments on a journey from ancashire to the North-East. After nloading at Seal Sands, its back load of 23 ns of caustic soda fills the centre ompartment for the homeward haul. Pete avison is one of the regular drivers of this ard-working Roadtrain.

Scammell was far too heavy. He persevered for a fortnight before he took it into the workshops where it was discovered that the steering was alright, it was just that there was no grease on the big fifth-wheel coupling so consequently the semi-trailer didn't want to bend.

Another well remembered pair of Scammells were a couple of the Trunker IIs that had the semi-automatic gearbox. The system was ideal in theory but was plagued by drivers who wouldn't 'toggle up' every morning (move the gear shift 20 times between each of the five gears) so consequently they complained that the bands always needed adjustment. Fuel consumption on these two was also rather poor, with 4 to 5mpg being all that could be expected. The two were also capable of going off on their own, as driver Arthur Wilcox discovered one day: he drove into the yard and, thinking no more about it, leapt out of the Scammell only to see it drive off into the garage wall because he had failed to knock it out of drive.

What the artic concept did give to Gilbraiths, and all other operators at the time, was an increase in weight limits when compared to the eight-wheeler. The Leyland Lynx was tried up to about 26 tons gross but wasn't a great success and the Leyland Buffalos, with their fixed-head engines, were great when they were running well but a big headache when they went off song. The Marathons found far better favour but Gilbraiths also continued to use Scammells – the last being the Crusaders – until the T45 Roadtrains came into use about 1980.

The period of recession in the early 1980s hit Gilbraiths like many others but the last ten years has seen them emerge in a more healthy vein. The change up to 38 tonnes in 1983 was an option that Gilbraiths welcomed and Chris

Chaplow, who now heads up day-to-day operation oversees a fleet predominantly run at this level. The line almost identical Leylands does conceal five very speci outfits which Gilbraiths are naturally very pleased about. problem in hauling chemicals is created by the b variations in their specific density. 'The Popemobile', as th first special semi-trailer was nicknamed, gets round th problem and is able to haul two different products on th two legs of a round trip without either contamination overloading. A three-compartment tank has the first an third compartments loaded up to the gross weight wit ethylene dichloride which is hauled from Seal Sands o Teesside across to Lancashire. The same vehicle, afte unloading, then fills up the central compartment, again the maximum 38 tonnes gross, with much heavier causti soda liquor for the return trip from Lancashire back acros to Teesside. Starting off in January 1988, this concept ha since spread to five similar outfits which are run six days week on a double-shift basis.

The red-painted Rolls-Royce-powered Roadtrains no head Gilbraiths' march into the 1990s, a quintet interloping ERFs being bought when the company of J.I Mitchell was acquired in 1988. All the fleet vehicles were t come under new ownership in 1990 when the share previously owned by Simon Engineering were bought ou The new owner of the business is Gilton Ltd which, as th name suggests, is a partnership between John Gilbraith an Derek Pilkington, respectively son and son-in-law of Phili Gilbraith. So in essence, after a break of 34 years, Gilbrait Tankers is now fully owned by the descendants of Henr Gilbraith – he can have had little idea back in 1920 how fa that original stake of £500 would take the company.

Fleet list

Gilbraith Tankers Ltd

ERF 'C' series

Fleet no	Reg no	Fleet no	Reg no	Fleet no	Reg no
112	B665 RNC	153	A893 MFV	174	E26 KFR
113	C225 CBA	154	A809 NCW	175	E134 NBV
		155	A445 PRN	176	E133 NBV
ERF 'E' series		156	B219 UBV	177	F116 VFV
		157	B239 XFV	178	F115 VFV
Fleet no	Reg no	158	B238 XFV	179	F226 BFV
114	D173 ONA	159	C979 FBV	180	F227 BFV
115	D311 RNC	160	C980 FBV	181	G942 GRN
116	E481 JCX	161	C981 FBV	182	G949 GRN
		162	C274 JFV	183	G932 GRN
Leyland Roadtrain 4x2		163	C275 JFV	184	G942 HRN
		164	C276 JFV	185	G941 HRN
Fleet no	Reg no	165	D308 UFV	186	G52 NFV
145	A985 JBV	166	D435 VCW	187	G49 NFV
146	A986 JBV	167	D611 AFV	188	G637 KBV
147	A984 JBV	168	E982 FCW	189	H647 VHG
148	A346 LCK	169	E582 JFR	190	H648 VHG
149	A347 LCK	170	E583 JFR	191	H227 XHG
150	A349 LCK	171	E733 MFV	192	unreg'd
151	A350 LCK	172	E734 MFV	193	H229 XHG
152	A454 LHG	173	E844 JHG		

2: J.R. Adams (Newcastle) Ltd

It's not surprising that Tyneside has spawned so many well-known names in the history of transport. The area has a rare mixture of specialized industry producing everything from tanks to tin cans, chemicals to car panels and paint to paper handkerchiefs, so naturally the people who move this great diversity of traffic have had to adapt to its many special needs. Not everyone has been able to live with the ever-changing face of Geordie-land and some of the area's once famous hauliers have just slipped away into the archives of history. J.R. Adams (Newcastle) Ltd, however, is one long-established family concern which still continue to provide the same high standard of transport service that they have offered for over 60 years with no sign that anything is set to change.

Currently based in large, covered premises at Longrigg, Swalwell, just off Newcastle's A69 western by-pass, Adams run a premium fleet of close to 40 strong. With the emphasis on articulation, traction favours the three-axled motive unit, and the fleet flagships are Leyland Roadtrain and ERF-based. It has been an Adams priority to 'fly the flag' and buy British whenever possible, a formula, like their traditional maroon livery, which is perhaps refreshing in these days of power and glitz. But you can't survive in this game on tradition alone: the Adams answer is to give a good service and work very hard at it into the bargain. The example of what is needed comes very much from the top. Now well into his ninth decade, company founder James Robertson Adams has a daily routine which would unsettle many. Into the depot by 7.30am, six days a week, it's generally ten hours later before he thinks about going home. Sunday may be a later start but it isn't a day off to this effervescent octogenarian – the family transport fleet is certainly a huge part of his life.

'Jakey', as he is normally called, is not the only James Adams at Longrigg for his son also has the same name. 'Young Jimmy' might be a glowing term for a 58-year-old but you can run out of variations when you learn that one of his two sons shares the name too. Like his brother John, James the youngest and father Young Jimmy run the traffic and administration side of the company, with grandfather Jakey still very much at home and involved with the engineering side of his fleet.

Naturally, Jakey started off with a single-horsepower vehicle. Living on Morley Street, Byker, in the eastern suburbs of Newcastle, Adams ran a coal business round the local back-to-back houses with a horse and cart. Not the biggest of frames, Jakey was renowned for one of the strongest hearts going. The story goes that, once his horse had tired for the day it could relax in the stable with its feed, whilst Jakey worked the streets by himself, harnessed to the shafts of the cart. If he wasn't delivering coal or carting round the East End, he was probably out selling newspapers, or doing anything else to scratch a living and build up a stake. He was determined to progress, and by the mid-1930s the horse and cart had gone and a Model A Ford had come in its place – the foundation of J.R. Adams was definitely being laid.

The path he was set to follow wasn't rock-free, but with the arrival of wartime years, the structuring of the MOWT – Ministry of War Transport – meant regular paid work for the hard-grafting Adams. The early 1940s also saw Jakey get together with George Thomas and Joe Bell, an alliance that is still together 46 years on. George had also been running a coal business in Newcastle but financial struggles prompted him to throw his hand in and, together with young 16-year-old Joe, he went to work for Jakey up at Byker Park.

With somebody to work alongside him that he could totally rely on, Jakey now looked to develop his fleet of two Commers into something more substantial. For an office, George Thomas went down to Chester-le-Street with one of the Commers and returned to Union Road, Byker with

This Atkinson, AJR 618, was one of the vehicles with which Adams set up again – officially – when BRS began selling off some of their stock. It was bought at a sale in Newcastle (unlike a whole group which came from Manchester) and is believed to have started life in 1945 with Armstrongs of Gateshead. Its appearance belied its age, for Adams had the vehicle totally refurbished by Atkinson before putting it on the road. Regular driver was Charlie Quickfall, recalled as always being able to get a bit more go out of the Atky's Gardner 6LW engine.

an ex-Northern single-deck bus body perched precariously on the back. With some of the seats thrown out, it was ideal. To show he had really arrived in the transport world, Jakey skinted himself by throwing all his money into JTN 556, a brand-new ERF four-wheeler. Not content with getting at least seven tons of payload on to the new motor, Jakey also put five tons on to a drawbar trailer, and places like Cardiff, London, Lancashire or Glasgow became regular destinations for the 'wagon and drag'. Having only the five-cylinder Gardner engine – all the six-potters were saved for front-line war-vehicles – the ERF wasn't really a greyhound but Jakey lovingly cosseted his latest acquisition. Jackie Hughes was the regular trailer mate for the outfit and he recalls that Jakey drove extremely steadily, at no more than

20mph. With a considerate position tight into the nearside kerb, you thought he was going to knock all the lamposts down, he passed them that close.

There was little comparison between the ERF and the earlier Commers. The latter were supplied by local dealer Minories and, at £654 a time, complete with body and sign-written, they were certainly cheap. But put any more than five tons on them and braking was a nightmare. The fleet was set to expand, with a Perkins P6-powered Vulcan coming and another brand-new ERF four-wheeler, LVK 218. This one ran solo as it only had the 4LW engine. Also bought new were a batch of Seddon four-wheelers. The Tyneside dealer for this marque was, strangely, the CWS (Co-operative Wholesale Society) at St Mary's Place so, as

OTY 262 joined the fleet in 1958, a fine example of the AEC Mustang with the 'Chinese Six' wheel arrangement. This photograph shows the vehicle near one of Manchester's main stations, the city being a regular calling place for the Adams wagons. Billy Craig was the regular driver of this vehicle and he is remembered as being a good grafter. The Mustang was well thought of too, a 'canny wagon', but when running light had trouble getting a grip on slippery roads.

Had it not been for the diligent record of the J. R. Adams fleet in the late 1950s and 1960s kept by photographer Roger Kenney, this chapter would have lacked its first six fine illustrations. Here, in Manchester again, he has captured an Albion Reiver and, behind it, a 1959 AEC Mammoth Major, MNL 359. The Albion's regular driver was Sal Turnbull, a native of Prudhoe, whose distinctive walk earned him the permanent nickname 'Happy Feet'.

well as purchasing groceries and furniture, you could also buy a wagon through the Co-op to move them, although in fact the Adams men tended to go down to Oldham and collect the new vehicles themselves straight from the factory.

The growing fleet had just reached double figures in time to clash with the new Labour government's programme of nationalization. Many people found this period difficult but to Jakey Adams it was worse than that. He vowed that no-one was going to re-possess his treasured wagons and, were it not for the local police accompanying the government officials, there might well have been more than just raised voices. The local representative of the law calmed Jakey down and pointed out that he really couldn't do anything about the situation. Adams may have accepted the money but he decided he was definitely going to get his own back and not let 'the Labour' get away with it.

What Jakey did was clearly illegal but, in fairness, he wasn't the only one who 'pirated'. When his fleet of 12 disappeared out of the door, he went out and bought a couple of old wagons including a Foden eight-wheeler. Painting them BRS red, but leaving his name off, meant that they looked like virtually every other wagon on the road and didn't attract unwelcome attention. Whilst officially they were vehicles that were to be used for internal factory work only, thus not requiring carriers' licences, Adams took a chance and worked at the job that he loved. It may be easy to look back and criticize Jakey's actions in this period but before you do, you really have to try and understand his feelings. Ever since being a lad, he had worked relentlessly in his chosen field of transport. He had always been his own man, knowing nothing else and, even though the government said he couldn't run long distance, it was not a law that he agreed with nor did he feel that it was morally fair. Adams thought it out and took the risk for his beliefs. Although he managed to live on his wits for a couple of years and run without proper licences, it was a huge relief when denationalization was announced.

Adams went to Manchester to buy his first lots of ex-

Joe Bell waxes lyrical over his old AEC Marshal double-drive six-wheeler, which he got new in 1964. Recalled as a particularly good puller, its 7.7-litre engine would take it up to over 50mph and it returned 9 or 10mpg. Hidden beneath the sheets is about 14 tons of bacon, a regular cargo for the Adams fleet. Joe's previous drive had been an older Mammoth Major, 219 JTN, fleet number 76.

Twenty-five years on, this photograph has completely flummoxed the Adams family because they cannot understand how their AEC Mandator came to be coupled to a tanker semi-trailer, a type of load carrier which they did not possess. This AEC, with the 9.6-litre engine and six-speed gearbox, was not common but was well liked in the mid-1960s, and remembered for its good brakes. The driver is identified as Sammy Swales, but if anyone knows how or why he was pulling a tanker, the head office at Swalwell would like to hear from you!

Opposite: Company founder James Robertson Adams – or Jakey, as he's more usually called – is seen in his preferred mode of dress among his much loved Scammell Crusaders, motors he wouldn't have anything said against.

BRS vehicles by tender, setting up again – officially – with about 16 assorted vehicles. Seddon and Leyland dominated this mixture although there was also a Maudslay 'Chinese Six' and a Foden six-wheeler having only single tyres on the rearmost of the two back axles. It was to be Lancashire and the North-West that J.R. Adams were to specialize in, re-establishing a pre-nationalization pattern of traffic. Chemicals from Washington Chemical Company plus bagged zinc oxide had taken the fleet in that direction, whilst a lot of back-loading had been asbestos sheets from Turners at Widnes and Manchester.

Such was the dominance of this pattern of work that an office was established at Blackfriars, Manchester, to co-ordinate back loads. Working in the office back at Byker was 'Young Jimmy' who, after his national service and a short learning time with BRS, came into the company, finding that his role was a far more varied one than it had been in the regimented BRS. At Adams, even the office man was expected to shunt the early-morning wagon, back from Lancashire, or even run down to Wetherby to do a quick change-over with some urgent traffic to deliver. The underlying emphasis for all the Adams team was to keep the

This was one of the first examples of the Scammell Handyman that Adams took into service. It had the Leyland 680 engine and is seen coupled to a 30ft Crane Fruehauf semi-trailer. Sammy Swales was the regular driver of this wagon and its load in this case is believed to be from Turners of Henley Green, Wigan, who were regular Adams customers.

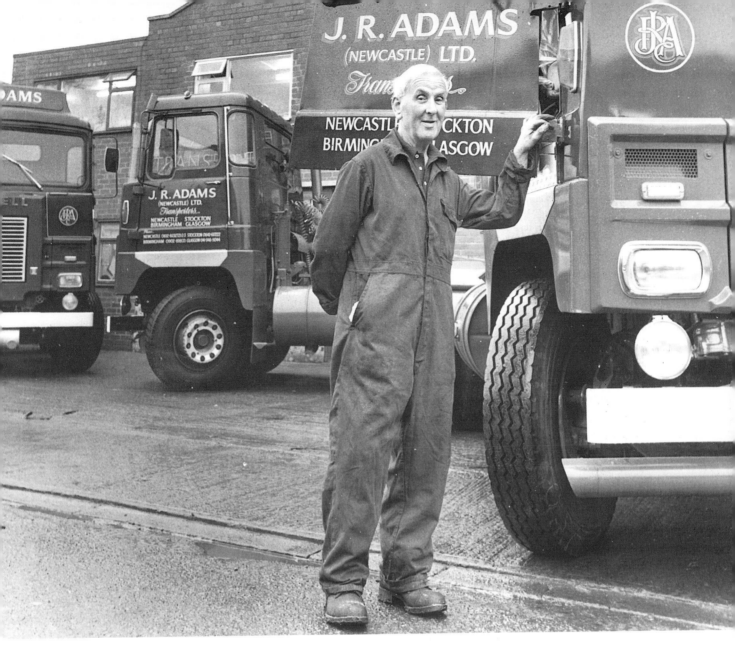

vehicles going. George Thomas seemed to spend all his time on the road repairing one wagon or another and even getting brand-new Bedfords as replacements for the BRS hand-me-downs didn't seem to make his life any easier. Supplied by Adams & Gibbons, the S-types came with the Perkins R6 engine – and they also came with an awful habit of throwing the timing chain off.

In search of bigger payload, the newly introduced Albion Reivers were bought. Joe Bell remembers learning about a strange idiosyncrasy with this six-wheeler. He was just passing Doncaster Racecourse one day and couldn't really understand why everybody else was flashing him. A look in the mirror revealed some smoke from behind but he didn't think he was in any trouble until he stopped and found the whole back end of the Albion on fire. Like this one, another Reiver was to be totally burnt out before Adams realized how critical tyre matching was on the Albion's rear bogie. You couldn't fit one brand-new tyre amongst the set of eight on the back end, for if you did, the slight difference

in sizes between the new and worn tyres meant the wheels would revolve at slightly different speeds and so generate a massive heat build-up in the final drive. So the invention of the third differential was one thing that J.R. Adams welcomed.

By the late 1950s, it was the AEC Mammoth Majors that were their particular Kings of the Road. All were adorned in the standard maroon livery, the gold-leaf signwriter of old being Effie Fenwick who only charged £15 per vehicle, which even included two coats of varnish. Jock Scott was given one of the new Mammoth Majors, and his vehicle was recalled as being one of the few seven-wheelers ever seen in use. Stopping one night near Wetherby to answer the call of nature, he went to climb down from the cab only to realize that his front offside wheel complete with stub axle and drum was completely missing. Unbeknown to Jock, he had shed it some way back up the A1 but fortunately the errant wheel was spotted by two BRS drivers as it careered over the dual carriageway in front of them. Returning it down

Many thanks for a
Job well done.
Jock Boyd.

e road to Jock from that far-off field made it a lengthy
pair but at least fitter Thomas had the original bits to
ork with and the cost of the incident was minimized.
Jock was on the telephone again over another incident at
etherby when he rang in to report that the small prop
aft which ran between the first and second drive axles had
me adrift. 'Where's the prop shaft now?' asked the bleary-
ed Thomas down the phone, to be told that it was two
iles away at Collingham. This seemed impossible, as
eorge knew that the AEC would quickly come to a stop
ce that prop shaft had come off. It did, of course, stop
irly abruptly but before Jock could retrieve the prop shaft
om the road, an E-type Jaguar ran over it. The Jag's
iver wasn't very happy about the damage this might have
used to his underside so, in exchanging particulars, he

posite: dwarfed by a crane at Blyth
arbour, RRG 524S is at the end of an
erland haul from Southampton in about
80. Billy Glendinning was the driver of
is 'B' series ERF with Rolls-Royce 265
wer which was coupled to a variable-
ngth 40 to 60ft Crane Fruehauf semi-
ailer. Jock Boyd was the proud owner of
is old 15-ton lifeboat and was to convert
into a Northumberland-based fishing
ssel. Adams subsequently disposed of
ailer number 4, but similar extendibles 5
d 7 are still in service.

ictured at the Hargreaves depot in Team
alley, Gateshead, during 1983, salesman
lan Stokoe, left, is handing a young
oking James Adams the keys for three of
ur identical Roadtrain 4x2 32-tonners,
ith Cummins-Fuller transmissions,
hich were delivered together. Adams
ave long had a policy of buying in batches
nd then storing prior to use. Consequently
378 YNL never ran with that number and
as subsequently registered B405 ENL.
arry Amos is the regular driver of that
eyland, whilst 379 usually has Laurence
auxwell behind the wheel.

lso declared that he would retain this lump of metal as
evidence' before he disappeared off home to Collingham. It
ook a visit from the local constabulary at 3 o'clock in the
norning to the car driver's house and the threat of a theft
harge against him before the vital shaft was retrieved.
    The cargo being hauled that night was a load of Danish
acon, an Adams regular, for most of this traffic was routed
nto the UK via the Tyne and the Newcastle quayside. It
vas imperative that the AEC didn't waste much time at
Wetherby for no matter how long it took to get your 150
ales of hessian-wrapped bacon on to your flat back, Jock
knew it had to be delivered first thing the next morning.
There were always plenty of customers for the 15 types of
mported bacon, but Young Jimmy recalls that a product
called Onam wasn't as successful. Adams were to transport
and store 28,000 cases of this imported ham and pork
mixture only to have to return it to the docks for

reshipment when the salesman couldn't sell a single tin.
    Such a big quantity created a storage problem, even
though the company had moved in about 1964 to a new
garage in Fisher Street, Walker. The vehicles in service
were also on the change as trials with a second-hand AEC
Mandator introduced the company to the joys of
articulation. But it wasn't AECs that were taken into use in
the end: a phase of cooling-system troubles encouraged
Jakey to change horses to the Scammell Handyman. All the
modern vehicles that Adams have used have neither been
subsequently sold nor even traded in part-exchange. Jakey's
doctrine of staying with a vehicle if it did you well meant
that it was possible to cannibalize and use up pieces of your
old, redundant vehicles. Bits were sold to other hauliers too,
as models began to change, with the Rolls-Royce-powered
Crusader eventually replacing the Leyland 680-powered
Handyman.
    All fleet vehicles were now travelling further afield, with
an office created in Glasgow to manage the vast number of
casting back loads that Adams moved. Bristol too generated
a lot of north-eastern bound zinc ingots. By 1975, J.R.
Adams reached their peak fleet size, running about 50
vehicles. A request by the mining engineers Huwood Ltd to
take over their entire traffic and also their own-account fleet
of 12 prompted this big rise in numbers but ample work
was found for this influx from the huge steel-plate mills at
Hartlepool. The late 1970s was a boom time for Adams,
moving anything up to 400 tons a day out of Hartlepool
alone. But the recession of the early 1980s, coupled to the
closure of the Hartlepool plate mill, forced a reduction
down to their current size of between 30 and 40 vehicles.
    The 38-tonnes legislation was found to be ideal for the

At Swalwell in January 1991, Joe Bell is about to drop a cargo of shipyard chains. This was one of a dozen identical loads hauled b
Adams, each tipping the scales at about 22 tons, from the auction site at the old Austin & Pickersgill yard in Sunderland down to Widnes
Joe, now into his fifth decade with Adams, speaks very highly of his Cummins-powered Roadtrain which is more usually used for shuntin
duties round the North-East.

steel traffic. Jakey preferred the twin-steer type of three-axled tractor unit at this sort of weight band. Cummins, first at 290 and then 320bhp, was the preferred power for the Scammell-built Roadtrains but when the DAF influence grew too strong, Adams reverted to buying 6x2 ERFs with similar engines. In 1984, the company moved to their current base, the old Ellis Steel fabrication works in Swalwell. It has proved to be highly suitable for warehousing and even garaging for the whole fleet. All vehicles are now fitted with cab phones, removing the need for those offices at Manchester, Glasgow and Billingham.

Some of the traffic currently being moved comes from customers like Tyneside Tin Printers who have entruste J.R. Adams with their wares for over 50 years. Other traffic like Danish bacon and butter has disappeared into containerized fridge vehicles, whilst a massive amount o work was lost when large parts of Vickers Engineering were bulldozed to the ground. But the changing times on Tyneside haven't brought any change in the Adams attitude of old. Supported by family and long-serving staff alike Jakey has always said that if you gave him the job, then you knew the job would be done.

The ERF six-wheeler with the 14-litre Cummins 320 engine has now taken over the mantle of Adams flagship. G21 VJR, photographed at Swalwell in February 1991, is the regular steed of Mick Findley, known because of his size as 'Moby Dick'. The Crane Fruehauf semi-trailer is one of eight curtainsiders on the Adams fleet, in this case laden with beer for delivery into the London area.

Fleet list

J. R. Adams (Newcastle) Ltd

Reg no	Chassis no	Make/model	Axles	Type*
WPT 799R	33702	ERF	4x2	A
UEU 385T	3766	ERF	4x2	A
VJR 536T	–	Scammell Crusader		B
XBB 995T	243880	Ford 'D'	4x2	FH
BPT 377V	105789E	Leyland	4x2	F
MBB 387X	05850	Mercedes-Benz	4x2	A
FNA 473Y	75433	Seddon Atkinson	4x2	R
A379 YNL	RLJE30846	Leyland Roadtrain	4x2	A
B404 ENL	RLJE30581	Leyland Roadtrain	4x2	A
B405 ENL	RLJE30586	Leyland Roadtrain	4x2	A
B406 ENL	RLJE30837	Leyland Roadtrain	4x2	A
B86 ETY	256701	DAF	4x2	R
C156 AOU	62256	Ford Cargo	4x2	R
C779 YWS	56819	Ford Cargo	4x2	R
C780 YWS	56820	Ford Cargo	4x2	R
C403 KTY	SEF76930	Leyland Roadtrain	6x2	A
D849 TJR	70982	Leyland Roadtrain	6x2	A
D851 TJR	70115	Leyland Roadtrain	6x2	A
D852 TJR	70078	Leyland Roadtrain	6x2	A
E484 ATY	71083	Leyland Roadtrain	6x2	A
E485 ATY	70983	Leyland Roadtrain	6x2	A
E486 ATY	71226	Leyland Roadtrain	6x2	A
E973 FJR	57309	ERF	6x2	A
E974 FJR	58068	ERF	6x2	A
F707 JCN	CJ12213	Leyland Freighter	4x2	T
F708 JCN	DJ12975	Leyland Freighter	4x2	R
F709 JCN	DJ13523	Leyland Freighter	4x2	R
F710 JCN	DJ13394	Leyland Freighter	4x2	R
F711 JCN	DJ72886	Leyland Roadtrain	6x2	A
F712 JCN	CJ72765	Leyland Roadtrain	6x2	A
F764 MNL	62844	ERF	6x2	A
F765 MNL	62532	ERF	6x2	A
F767 MNL	63286	ERF	6x2	A
F768 MNL	–	ERF	4x2	R
G916 JBB	62542	ERF	6x2	A
G21 VJR	64539	ERF	6x2	A
G22 VJR	65462	ERF	6x2	A
G23 VJR	65532	ERF	6x2	A

*Types: A artic tractor unit; B breakdown unit; F flat; H Hiab; R rigid; T Tautliner.

13: Thomas Allen Ltd

Walk down Victoria Road in the idyllic-sounding Essex town of Stanford-le-Hope and you might see a small slice of history: affixed to the side of an unassuming doorway is a brass plate bearing the words 'Thomas Allen Ltd Registered Office'. That piece of metal, plus the memories of many, is all that remains of a transport fleet that once ran close to 300 strong. For Thomas Allen's tankers, at least in their own identity, are a thing of the past, as they now form a major component of P&O Roadtanks Ltd. With its head office at Station House in Altrincham, Cheshire, P&O Roadtanks now embraces 1,000 tank trailers, 500 tank containers and 800 tractor units which operate from a chain of 13 UK depots. Across in Continental Europe, the company is active in Holland, Belgium, Austria and Germany, its business the carriage of bulk liquids, both hazardous and non-hazardous, powders and gases, all moved in a fashion that is quality assured.

It was from January 1, 1990, that the name of Thomas Allen Ltd was officially no more, its place taken by the new corporate image of P&O Roadtanks. But those who mourned its passing knew that it was a belated one, the result of a change in policy away from the parent company's earlier practice of retaining the identities of the transport concerns it had absorbed in its more recent history. Thomas Allen Ltd had been acquired as far back as 1971 but, just as with its sister subsidiaries A. S. Jones, Haley Bros, James Hemphill, John Foreman and Robert Armstrong, the name had continued to be used both on the vehicles and in all the paperwork.

P&O had been unusual in this respect. The more general trend had been for medium and even large tanker operators, once bought out by a larger conglomerate, rapidly to lose the original haulier's name. To enthusiasts and followers of the road-transport scene, 'under new management' normally indicated that yet another name was shortly destined to disappear. P&O had bucked that trend for,

although their extensive fleet all shared the same Olympic Blue and white livery, the cab-door lettering continued to specify an individual operating company. The one drawback, as far as operations went, was that road tankers had tended to be rather localized vehicles, so that whilst the name of Allens might be very well known in London and the South-East, it wasn't instantly recognizable in Scotland or north-east England. The same went for A. S. Jones or for Hemphills: once you moved out of their own particular heartlands, the influence of their traditions and reputation was lost. Inevitably, then, the common owner, P&O, had to come to the fore. The name was well enough established in the shipping world, and the gradual growth of the road transport operation over 20 years finally peaked at the point where the old names were cut away and P&O Roadtanks stood alone.

As one of the leaders in putting the road-tanker business on its feet, Thomas Allen Ltd will perhaps be missed more than some. The impartial historian may reflect, however, that the name had been living on borrowed time and even that it could easily have disappeared completely 92 years ago, for the earliest days of the firm weren't by any means the smoothest. Both organizations, Allen and its modern day parent P&O, have roots in the mid-19th century, albeit in a different sphere of transport.

It was in 1837 that an Englishman, Brodie McGhie Wilcox, and a Shetlander, Arthur Anderson, who ran a shipping service between London and the Iberian Peninsula, won their first deep-sea mail contract. On December 31, 1840, their Peninsular and Oriental Steam Navigation Company was incorporated by royal charter giving birth to one of the most famous names in shipping. Egypt, India, the Far East and Australia were now on the P&O itinerary – exotic stuff compared with the origins of Thomas Allen's firm.

He too started in London and, in 1854, founded his

...tage business at leased stables in Great Hermitage Street,
...Georges, Middlesex, nowadays known as Hermitage
...all, Wapping, London E1. The rent of £48 per annum
...s paid to James Hartley & Co who occupied both the
...itish & Foreign Steam Wharf and Millers Wharf in
...wer East Smithfield. Hartley's provided Thomas Allen
...th an office on the wharf and the operation of cartage was
...n almost on a contract basis with Allen doing the work
...stigated by the Hartley business. James Hartley & Co had
...multitude of interests, being agents to the British & Irish
...eam Packet Co and to the City of Cork Steam Packet Co.
...ith this strong link to Ireland, it's not surprising to learn
...at Hartleys were the London managers for Arthur
...uinness, Son & Co, the famous Dublin brewers. Their
...rk nectar was shipped from Dublin to London by the
...itish & Irish Steam Packet Co, their ships being unloaded
...erside on to barges near Millers Wharf. The barges
...ansferred it to dry land and it was then the task of
...homas Allen's carts to deliver this distinctive drink to the
...uinness customers in London.

The huge barrels of Guinness weren't the only traffic of
...is carter as everything which passed through the

Things got so bad that the company came up for disposal
by the Court of Chancery.

The links that Thomas Allen had forged with James
Hartley had been particularly strong. So, knowing of the
carters' potential, William Turner, who was in the Inwards
Department of Hartley's, bought the business of Allens in
1898 at terms dictated by the Court. Even though the firm
was about as far down as it could possibly go, Turner wasn't
going to throw away the reputation of 50 years' trading, so
the name of Thomas Allen was kept for this cartage
business. Turner took on as a junior partner one William
Bass, his foreman horse keeper, and it was to be the families
Turner and Bass which lifted Thomas Allens back to a
more creditable state. Their success would ensure the
continuity of the name as the early 1900s heralded a big
change in affairs.

James Hartley were dealt a number of body blows in the
early years of the new century: first, in 1911, Arthur
Guinness set up their own organization and thus no longer
needed the Hartley management, though they still made use
of the Allens carts direct. In 1914, Hartleys also lost the
agency of the British & Irish Steam Packet Co as this had

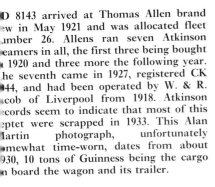

...D 8143 arrived at Thomas Allen brand
...ew in May 1921 and was allocated fleet
...umber 26. Allens ran seven Atkinson
...eamers in all, the first three being bought
...1920 and three more the following year.
...he seventh came in 1927, registered CK
...44, and had been operated by W. & R.
...cob of Liverpool from 1918. Atkinson
...cords seem to indicate that most of this
...eptet were scrapped in 1933. This Alan
...artin photograph, unfortunately
...mewhat time-worn, dates from about
...930, 10 tons of Guinness being the cargo
...n board the wagon and its trailer.

...harfinger business of Hartleys was probably hauled by
...llen's carts. Thomas Allen achieved the important status
...f Bonded Carmen Contractor. Although little more is
...nown of these earlier days, it is clear that the founder ran
...he firm until his death sometime after 1872.

Interest in his firm was left to his widow, Annie Lydia
...llen, and his daughter, Mrs Ryan, with the day-to-day
...management entrusted to John Kingston, a superintendent
...f Millers Wharf. The structuring of the business was
...lightly strange in that Kingston paid the owners a flat rate,
...hat to Mrs Ryan being £25 per month, for the right to
...operate the company. Kingston took advantage of his new
...post by being brought from home in Bow Road to Millers
...Wharf each morning in a four-wheeled cab driven by
...William Bateman, one of Allen's carmen. But Kingston's
...management of affairs wasn't as grand as his aspirations and
...n the late 1890s the Allen business began to go downhill.

been bought by Coast Lines Ltd. So, capitulating to the
tide, their interests were merged with that of Coast Lines
Ltd. The business shake-up continued when, in 1920, the
Turner family sold their cartage business to Coast Lines:
the creation of Thomas Allen Ltd, as a separate entity, saw
Philip Turner, son of William Turner, take the post of
Managing Director.

Whilst all these transfers of ownership were taking place,
the method of haulage adopted by Allens was also on the
change. They became quite excited, like many, about the
developments with the internal combustion engine but very
frustrated too with its unreliability factor. So although the
use of the horse and cart still predominated, the Allen fleet
received an influx of steamers, conferring the benefits of
mechanization with greater reliability than the infant petrol
engine could offer. Hauling drawbar trailers, the steamers
could handle payloads, especially the heavy Guinness

Tricana was one of many customers that Thomas Allen used to haul for on a contract basis, and these three vehicles indicate the wid variety of chassis which they used for tanker work in the early days. The Scammell Rigid 8, which dates from 1946, was remembered f needing reinforcement around the tank at the point where it sat above the rubber-sprung bogie. In the centre is a 1944 12LA tractor un and on the right is fleet number 325, registered FYM 662, a Leyland Beaver four-wheeled rigid which dates from 1940.

barrels, up into unprecedented double figures. Allens were to run a total of 30 steam wagons, made up of four Taskers, six Fodens, 13 Sentinels and seven Atkinsons.

But, just as with the horse-drawn cart, there were drawbacks to using steam power, including the dirt and grime associated with coal firing and the resultant ash, and the time it took to get up to working boiler pressure from a cold start. So it was something of a relief when motor manufacturers improved the quality of their products to an acceptable level. Allens' early purchases were a mixture of 30cwt and 50cwt Albions and, from the Government Disposal Board, First World War vehicles of assorted makes including Crossley, Peerless, Hallford, Loco, Riker and Pierce Arrow. Then, when Scammell Lorries of Watford announced their new articulated outfits in 1922, there soon began a relationship between Allens and Scammell that was to last unbroken for 50 years.

If the vehicles were developing, so too was Allens' working pattern. In 1920 they acquired the similar operations of Edmund Tanton Ltd which were based close at hand in Wapping High Street. Their parent, Coast Lines, was also on the acquiring trail and for a short time Kirks Cartage and Elder Dempster's Liverpool Cartage Company were known as Thomas Allen Ltd, Liverpool. Long-distance services were run for a few years between London, Portsmouth and Southampton. But the exciting move into tankers was occurring very much closer to home.

It was really the huge upsurge of the private motor car which in turn created the demand for the road tanker. Hauling petroleum fuel out from the refinery was an early job for Allens and they used solid-tyred J-type Thornycrofts which had 1,000-gallon tanks mounted on

their backs for these first bulk movements. Turpentine an fuel oil were also carried in bulk, but traffic like kerosen was very seasonal and so little use could be found for som tankers during the warmer summer months. Hauling suc volatile liquids meant there was no place for the tankers i the confines of Wapping and the outpost depot at Stanford le-Hope, in the wilds of Essex, was formed. To help justif its existence, the company's main engineering works wer also sited here under the banner of Stanford Engineerin Ltd: they too would form an important part of the story.

Back in the city, things were moving at a hectic pace New offices at 72–84, Hermitage Wall were occupied and i 1932 Allens took over the long-established wine and spiri cartage contractor, Henry Smither & Son. A thir subsidiary was acquired in August 1935, that being Henr Bourner, a cartage contractor who was responsible for th handling of 85% of London's hops on their way to th breweries. And brewing prompted the next big upheava for, in August 1934, Guinness announced they had built new brewery at Park Royal, London NW10. This mean that the Allen traffic in imported Guinness was eliminate but, having worked so closely for 80 years, the partnershi remained: Allens opened a garage at Park Royal and eve built 28 houses in Iveagh Avenue just for the drivers an mates to be near the job as the Guinness traffic not only changed but was expanded.

In the late 1930s, the traditional horses were still very much in use for local deliveries, but Allens were intereste in more modern forms of traction and began to work together with Scammell Lorries and Partridge Wilson wh were electrical engineers in Leicester. This co-operation, illustrating the far-sightedness of the company, resulted in

Albion Motors had first announced their model 127 in 1935 and by the time HGO 723 joined the fleet in 1946 the design was looking rather dated and overdue for transformation into the Chieftain. Jatex was a brand name for Dunlop's latex, and Allens carried a lot of this product out of Liverpool for subsequent use in carpet manufacture. The photograph shows the Albion just having been rebuilt after a bad accident.

the design of an electric three-wheeled Mechanical Horse powered by batteries which could be charged up overnight. Seven of these were taken into service after 1937, with some success. They proved comparable to a pair of horses, being able to haul the same four-ton load, and they had a range between charges approaching 30 miles, with a laden top speed of 10mph.

This mechanical flair was further developed during World War 2 as Stanford Engineering Ltd, under the consultant eye of famous Scammell man Percy G. Hugh, worked for the Ministry of Aircraft Production, reportedly the only haulier in the country to become a direct contractor. It was then down to the men and (mainly) the women of Thomas Allens to manufacture a wide variety of products like cradles capable of accommodating launches up to 78ft long, special boat hooks, air cleaners for desert use by the army, heavy transporter axles and component parts for prefabricated Bailey bridges.

Life in Essex was a picnic in the wartime years when compared to that in London and Allens' interests around the dockland and Wapping received heavy bombing from the enemy. This prompted the decision to sell all the horses

This Malcolm Ladd photograph illustrates a type of outfit favoured by Allens for more than 20 years. Portrayed here at Stanford-le-Hope in 1947 just after entering service, HYP 370 was to be used mainly for Essex-based traffic on behalf of DCL and Chemi-trade. The Scammell tank semi-trailer ran on rubber suspension and the prominent hatch covers were insulated to conserve heat. Sister vehicle number 471 was a similar matched Scammell outfit, registered HYU 4.

This was one of eight similar 1949 Leyland Comets that were run out of Shellhaven on seasonal contract work. Power was a fuel company taken over by Shell, and the Leylands usually carried paraffin or gas oil on small deliveries to commercial premises and hospitals. During the warmer summer period these vehicles would be parked up for several months with no work to do.

before any were injured. Although the premises, vehicles and even one of the Guinness houses were severely damaged, dedication to duty by staff ensured that things were kept moving. It was a company instruction to all drivers that, should there be a German invasion, they must make their vehicles unusable in any way possible, and they were all issued with hammers for this purpose. The instruction was in the minds of Harry Beevers and Bill Anthony one day as they were travelling through South Wales when they encountered some German soldiers in a field next to the road. Quick as a flash, Harry stopped and

leapt out with the hammer to smash a huge hole in the side of the sump. Pleased to know that he had done his duty to comply with company instructions, it was with mixed feelings that he heard Bill explain that the 'Germans' were merely actors involved in the making of a propaganda film!

In 1945, Allens took over their fourth subsidiary in the form of Victoria Motor Haulage Co Ltd of 93, Wapping High Street, this haulier specializing in the movement of newsprint into the London-based newspapers like the *Daily Mail*. This added yet another item to the diverse portfolio of Thomas Allens' traffic: along with dock and wharf

Even though there was no sign of the Thomas Allen name on many of their contract vehicles, the fleet number roundel on the door and the Road Haulage Association badge were a sure indication of Allen ownership. Allens have always had and continue to have a big involvement with the RHA. Seen at Stanford-le-Hope, this 1950 AEC Mammoth Major is remembered as the only rigid six-wheeler in the fleet, the regular mount of driver Sam Skinner.

Running such a large fleet of tankers, Allens found themselves involved in moving an amazing variety of liquid products. These two Scammells, including number 687, registered SLP 281 and dating from 1956, are seen at Great Yarmouth loading apple juice for the well known cyder company, Gaymers. A number of vehicles were employed for this operation and the tanks had to be fitted with sealed tops to meet customs approval.

cartage, wines, spirits and hops, there was now newsprint, not forgetting of course the Guinness fleet and the growing band of tankers that were slowly multiplying out in Essex.

Being such a large concern, Thomas Allen seemed a natural to be swallowed up in the 1949 nationalization programme but in the event their unique structure saved them. The Guinness traffic was moved on 'C' hiring licences and was thus exempted, the intense Wapping work was all localized and thus also exempt, and whilst the Stanford-le-Hope-based vehicles ran further afield, tankers were also specifically exempted from legislation.

During the passage of time, the tanker interests had been slowly increasing so by 1954 there would be about 120 in service. This figure was to triple as Allens found themselves ideally structured to take on the massive growth in demand for bulk movements of liquid. You name it and probably Allens moved it, whether it was weedkiller, bitumen, soap, linseed or molasses. They even delivered fuel oil to South Stack lighthouse, Holyhead and similar oil to Hartland Point lighthouse via a pipeline laid under the sea.

Keeping track of Allens' vehicles became rather difficult as many tankers were based at a specific customer's factory and possibly painted in a contract livery with names like Regent Oil, Power Petroleum or Glaxo Laboratories

reflecting the wide variety of activity. All Allens' vehicles were painted under the supervision of foreman George Hockley and the mid-1950s costing of about £300 a time shows the care that went into each vehicle. Distillers Company were another concern that Allen hauled for and when DCL decided to adopt a new, bright green colour scheme, Allens decided to keep the previous DCL colours, which were a slightly lighter blue than their own dark shade, for themselves.

Allens had been obliged to use a variety of makes as work-horses. Smaller four-wheelers like Leyland Comets had been used for the seasonal paraffin work but, as the tanker boom took off, Allens opted to standardize on the maximum-weight four-axled artic at 22 and then 24 tons gross. They also standardized on Scammells and that marque became synonymous with Thomas Allens of Stanford-le-Hope, even though, as Frank Edwards recalls, the 15LA tractive units, which seemed to come in their hundreds, were priced at £2,760 each (a small fortune at that period) and you had to wait a long time for them, too.

As the 1950s positively boomed for Allens, the huge diversity of interests that the haulier was involved in demanded a complete re-assessment. Back in 1928, Arthur Bibby had been made Depot Manager at Stanford-le-Hope

This 1960 version of the Scammell Highwayman, registered 12 ALP, was fleet number 867. This particular vehicle was based at Gloucester and operated in a fashion known at Allens as 'double banked' the co-ordinated efforts of two local drivers ensured a non-stop service carrying emulsion between Treforest and the Wiggins Teape plant at Boreham Wood.

Towards the end of the 1960s, Allens were beginning to depart from their total reliance on Scammells for the tanker fleet, buying ERFs in greater numbers. At the request of the Chairman, two Seddon 32-ton tractor units were purchased as a trial but they weren't a complete success. There were problems with the front axle and brakes as well as with the Group rear axle. This stainless-steel semi-trailer tank had a capacity of 5,000 gallons.

and only needed to be there on a Tuesday and Thursday. The rest of the week was either spent out at customers or up at Wapping looking after the hop traffic. No one could have foreseen how things were to grow so fast, especially in the tanker field, so Thomas Allen in the 1950s is a company that should be remembered as it was one that, though successful, just had to be changed. The first thing to go was the Guinness traffic, hived off into Guinness' own transport fleet. The intense London operations, which had moved from Wapping to Canning Town, eventually underwent a huge restructuring. All the warehousing was to be embraced under a new company called Storemaster and, to cater for general haulage vehicles, the name of Henry Smither, taken over by Allens in 1932, was brought back into use. For its registered office, Thomas Allen Ltd moved out to Stanford-le-Hope. In turn, all these new arrangements were destined for yet more change when the parent of Allen/ Smither/Storemaster, Coast Lines Ltd, was in turn bought out by P&O in 1971. As we have seen, it took 19 years for P&O to absorb the Thomas Allen empire totally although the Smither and Storemaster names were quickly merged into P&O Roadways. Currently heading up P&O Roadtanks is Jim Paton, himself an ex-Thomas Allen man. So the name of Thomas Allen Ltd, which ended its days affixed to a fine fleet of tankers, is not yet forgotten, even if you can't find that unassuming doorway in Essex before the last clue is removed.

y the mid-1970s, imported DAF chassis
ad been adopted as the standard traction.
ut this Seddon Atkinson 400 was bought
pecifically for a five-year contract
ransporting the products of Phillips
etroleum who dictated that a British-
uilt tractor was a condition of the deal.
his outfit was first based at Thurrock,
ith John Chandler as its regular driver,
nd then later moved across to Ipswich.
he tank semi-trailer is still currently in
ervice.

Although all the P & O Group tanker
ompanies were eventually given a
niform colour scheme, the individual
aulier's name was still evident to even the
quickest of glances. 2068 is one of the well
iked DAF 2800s, seen running in its later
orm to take advantage of the 38-tonne
imit. The Ryland Tankers barrel was
originally built with a 5,500-gallon capacity
but, when the weight limit was raised, it
was cut open and stretched to 6,000 gallons.
The first conversions from two to three
trailer axles were accomplished by adding
a Granning lifting axle, but Dunlop
suspension was later preferred for this type
of uprating.

14: Highland Haulage Ltd

It was on September 30, 1986, that Highland Haulage ceased to exist as a company. The following day the vehicles, staff and premises became part of Connal Highland Ltd as two famous concerns, Connal & Co and Highland Haulage Ltd, both owned by the Transport Development Group, joined forces with a view to improving their corporate efficiency. But even now, when the telephone rings in the Inverness office, the caller's first question is sometimes 'Is that Highland Haulage?' It's apparent that even though the name and livery have changed, the links forged over 30 years between the transport customers of northern Scotland and the old identity of Highland Haulage mean that it will be many years yet before it's completely forgotten. Yet were it not for a twist of fate, the company might not have existed.

To trace the origin of Highland Haulage Ltd, you have to turn the clock back to the early 1950s and examine the activities of three particular British Road Services employees. George Wilson was at that time employed as Group Manager at Peterhead, Hector MacLennan was Group Manager at Inverness and William Wisely was District Manager at Aberdeen. All three were solid transport men, each having been involved extensively in road haulage prior to nationalization. George Wilson had in fact been manager at the old established concern of Sutherlands in Peterhead before they were compulsorily acquired by BRS. But as the relaxations created by the partial denationalization of the BRS empire eventually arrived, George and his two colleagues decided to get together and make a bid for the entire Peterhead operations of BRS – no tendering for small lots of vehicles but a bid for the entire unit, lock, stock and barrel. In preparation for what they presumed would be a successful tender, they created the company of Sutherlands of Peterhead (Road Hauliers) Ltd in mid-1955, starting off the road fleet with seven or eight ex-BRS vehicles along with their respective licences, these obviously being intended as extras to the unit vehicles they were bidding for.

With so much lucrative fish traffic sourced out of Peterhead, they weren't the only people interested in this total acquisition, so as a back-up they also made a bid for the complete BRS Inverness depot. In truth, the latter was of little attraction to them as they knew from experience that making money out of haulage from that part of the Highlands was going to be plain hard work. As luck would have it the trio, always referred to as WMW, weren't successful with their bid for the Peterhead/Fraserburgh unit of BRS and it went to Charles Alexanders. A long-established concern in north-east Scotland, Alexanders had also been successful in buying the Old Ford Road BRS unit in Aberdeen which in essence had been the old Alexander depot prior to its nationalization in 1949. To say that George Wilson and his associates weren't happy in losing out to the Alexander bid would be putting it mildly, but on the positive side they learnt that they were successful in their bid for the BRS Inverness depot. This mix of circumstances left the WMW group in a bit of a quandary. To make a go of it at Inverness wasn't going to be easy, although with his local knowledge and good connections George Wilson could be fairly sure of attracting the vast majority of outward bound traffic from the Peterhead area. True, now only having seven or eight vehicles he couldn't think about moving all the traffic likely to be offered to him, but subcontracting on a substantial scale would ensure that things did get moved one way or another.

Since the company of Sutherlands of Peterhead had already been created, it was decided that the ex-BRS Inverness unit should be operated under the Sutherlands company but having the trading name of Highland Haulage Services. Although Alexanders had been successful in their bid at Peterhead, the amount of traffic actually handled by their services was extremely small, in fact so small that the hole future of the depot was called into question. It stuck their gullet rather to have to accept traffic on a contract basis from Sutherlands who really had far more loads than they could handle. While this situation continued it was a worrying time for Alexanders but it was resolved by getting together with the WMW group. All the parties involved knew each other very well so after detailed negotiations the decision was reached to incorporate all the vehicles based in the Peterhead area (those owned by Sutherlands and by Alexanders) into the company Sutherlands of Peterhead (Road Hauliers) Ltd. Ownership of this concern was to be split jointly between Alexanders and the WMW group and their associates.

The Inverness side of affairs wasn't involved in these negotiations so, with its would-be parent now sharing owners, the previously adopted trading name was dropped and the new company of Highland Haulage Ltd was formed in September 1955. Thus Highland Haulage was born on to the transport scene owning not only all of its own Inverness interests but also a 50% share in the fortunes of Sutherlands – Wilson, MacLennan and Wisely now in fact owned one and a half haulage concerns. George Wilson concentrated on managing the jointly-owned concern of Sutherlands, and Hector MacLennan took over the reins at Inverness. In practice, MacLennan had been managing here in BRS days so little had changed; in fact there were many people in the organization, like accountant Norman Smith, who had worked straight through from the days of Wordie, the haulier who was nationalized to form the BRS

Inverness unit. But back in the arena of a denationalized, competitive market place, the staff of the newly created Highland Haulage knew that they could no longer rely on the huge BRS empire to support them and they quickly had to learn how to stand on their own two feet. The Wordie business, continued by BRS, had been a mixture of fetching and carrying but always with the railhead as the focal point so that, although operations were of a hugely diverse nature, they were normally localized. But if Highland Haulage needed any impetus to broaden the horizons for their fleet of 40 or 50 vehicles, a timely rail strike meant that much long-distance traffic came to their doors and, receiving a very good service, many of those customers were never to leave them.

Given this opportunity, Highland Haulage quickly had to adapt to the changes demanded. No longer relying on the railways to run countrywide, it was the road fleet of Albions, Austins, Leylands, Seddons and then eventually AECs that was going to be relied on to cover the long-distance terrain. Inverness is 570 miles from London and it was up to people like George Harper, driving the fleet flagship Mammoth Majors, to punch ever southwards and champion his company. Highland Haulage ran 'wagon and drag' outfits on fish traffic with places like Grimsby, Hull and of course Pet Foods at Melton Mowbray being regular destinations. When Harper was hauling his Dyson drawbar trailer his regular mate was 'Nessie', who was of questionable age and a complete contrast to the other, far younger mates. George and Nessie fought like cat and dog

This scene in the old Longman Road depot in about 1959 illustrates how Highland Haulage kept the people of the Highlands region supplied with all of life's necessities. The loading docks with boards indicating various destinations from Wick and Thurso in the north to Grantown in the Spey valley to the south have a distinctly BRS look to them although in fact it was the long-established Inverness firm Wordie who had laid down this pattern of distribution work. The type of work, if not the terrain, emphasized the benefits of articulation which Highland Haulage were quick to adopt.

MST 521 was George Harper's regular AEC Mammoth Maj[or] seen here about 300 miles from home at rest while George tak[es] refreshment in the Croxdale Cafe on the old A1 just south [of] Durham city. The 11.3-litre AEC normally had a Dyson 'drag' [in] tow but is here running solo loaded with 'slabs' which were t[he] sections of timber left after the stripping process.

The name of Highland Haulage and the town of Inverness have [a] strong link which endures still, even though the company h[as] technically ceased to exist. Looking down on the town is B[ob] Campbell's 1958 Albion Reiver, known for its dearth of brake[s] loaded with a typical cargo of BOC bottles. Those interested w[ill] notice the horizontal loading and the size of the steel containers [of] 30 years ago, contrasting with the larger modern bottles which a[re] carried upright. Bob would probably tell you it just meant mo[re] to load and unload by hand.

but the driver could always upset the mate by one strange ritual: it wasn't unknown for him to unscrew the nut which held the steering wheel as he was driving along. Lifting the wheel clear of the column, he would push it across under the dozing mate's chin and frighten him into life with the cry 'Will you take the wheel, Nessie?'

The long-distance Highland Haulage men could reckon to be away from home roaming for anything up to three weeks before suitable traffic brought them back north. But by forming a chain of offices at Leith, Glasgow and Aberdeen, a structure of traffic flow both in and out of the Highlands was gradually built up. Gaining membership of the countrywide Transport Association, in whose creation Mr Wisely had been a driving force, was certainly a big

help: you have to be invited and accepted into the TA, it's not just a matter of applying. TA membership gave Highland Haulage access to back-load contacts as well as places that gave preferential refuelling and repair facilities.

What traffic there was available for Inverness and beyond was often given to Highland Haulage with thanks, because the prospect of going to far-flung outposts like Wick, Thurso or Ullapool made many of softer fabric simply shudder. In fact, the BRS Parcels organization continued to run trunk services for many years as far as Inverness but unloaded at Highland Haulage who then undertook the rest of the distribution. The reasoning behind this, apparently, was that they felt that working the Highlands region should be left to the people who knew it best. So it was partly just

Unlike many hauliers of the day, Highland Haulage never went in for an exuberant livery, incorporating a long list of depots and their telephone numbers which you could hardly read let alone remember – they felt that their name alone said it all. AECs were very highly thought of in the 1950s and '60s, this Mercury being coupled to a BTC four-in-line semi, a type of trailer remembered for its long life and low unladen weight. The Austin A35 sneaking into shot was the runabout for the Conan Bridge depot manager.

The Highlands of Scotland are famous for their outstanding beauty – and their extremes of weather. The drivers of old, who worked through some terrible conditions, did occasionally come to grief. This ERF in 1959 had made it almost 80 miles south down the old road before sliding off in the Pass of Killiecrankie. The cut timber it was carrying was loaded at Munros in Dingwall for delivery into England.

the surrounding terrain that gave Highland Haulage the right to be called the area's top dog. But their reputation didn't make it any easier for the drivers. Even now, the stories of Drumossie Brae still make the old salts shudder. That never-ending climb out on the old road southbound towards Perth meant that with an old Albion or even an AEC loaded to the gunnels, it would take at least an hour to claw your way up the first nine or ten miles of unrelenting mountainside. At times, drivers and mates ran with their doors open, not for air but just in case the vehicle didn't make it and you had to go for a quick exit.

But make it they did, not only over Drumossie but also in the business world, as the fortunes of Highland Haulage continued to prosper. They weren't the only Scottish haulier to ride the boom of a huge demand for Scottish fish and timber-related produce, so when the Transport Development Group went on the acquisition trail in the late

1950s, there were plenty to choose from. Charles Alexanders were the first in the area to be bought by TDG, which also meant that 50% of Sutherlands of Peterhead also came into that group's ownership. Sutherlands had thrived on the Peterhead fish traffic so, as TDG wanted total acquisition of this company as well, the lucrative offer to buy the remaining 50% share as well as Highland Haulage, in 1961, seemed too good for WMW to refuse.

Business continued as normal under new ownership although transitional effects included a depot move to the current Burnett Road site and W.A. Mackenzie taking over as Managing Director, both of which had their own significance. Whilst Longman Road had always been troubled with odd access niggles, Mackenzie's influence brought continued growth for Highland Haulage as it became the biggest haulier in Northern Scotland. Its leader also acquired a reputation for being quite a character. At

First introduced in 1960, the AEC Marshal was adopted by Highland Haulage following good service from the long-suffering Mammoth Majors. Inverness-based Billy Forbes is seen in this John Simons photograph near Aviemore during 1966 at the wheel of his brand-new six-legger which was one of the first Ergomatic Marshals operated in the north of Scotland. The vehicle, rated for a 24-ton gross weight, is fully loaded with bricks for delivery into Inverness.

times highly impatient, he wasn't averse, if one of his 90 drivers didn't turn in, to taking out a vehicle for delivery and collection work in the town of Inverness with Traffic Clerks like David Thomson with him to do the donkey work. If a sales representative wanted a conversation with the cigar-smoking MD, he would normally have to conduct it alongside an active fork lift truck as the boss showed that he could tackle anything his men were asked to do.

The portfolio of cargo that Highland Haulage carried was as varied as the community it served. Fish, timber, agricultural produce and BOC bottles were some of the main bulk traffic, as was whisky from the booming Spey Valley distilleries that Northern Scotland was renowned for. Destination of this valuable fluid was usually the bottling plants in the Central Belt and, before bulk handling by tanker was adopted, the golden nectar was moved in three different containers – barrels, hogsheads and bats. Whilst the ASBs (American Sized Barrel) contained 40 gallons and weighed in at about the 4cwt mark, the hogshead contained 55 gallons and tipped the scales at 5cwt. But this was lightweight compared to the bats that carried 110 gallons – they could break your back if you tried anything adventurous with that 10cwt lump.

The need for a regular run down to the Glasgow/Edinburgh regions led the company to instigate an overnight trunk, beginning with one vehicle. It is 178 miles from Inverness to Glasgow but, such was the terrible state of the A9 at that time, it was a good job just to do the

Like the Marshal, the AEC Mercury also gave sterling service to Highland Haulage, the company running about 20 of these Ergomatic-cabbed tractor units. John Simons caught fleet number 30 in the Fort William area, the York 36ft tandem-axled semi-trailer carrying a full load of building materials from Glasgow for delivery to Corpach. Roddy McKinnon is the man behind the wheel of the Mercury, this example being remembered for problems with the cylinder head gasket and the gearbox.

As the reputation of the AEC marque fell away, Highland Haulage quickly took to the Volvo F86 model, using it extensively in both rigid and articulated forms. This example was one of two artics subcontracted for work at Invergordon on Nigg Bay, loading steel pipes for the North Sea oil industry. The pipes were taken to be coated in cement before being laid on the sea bed to carry natural gas.

one-way run in a shift. But the A9 was going to improve and also on the change was the fleet make-up. The arrival of one of the first Volvos in Northern Scotland, an F86 6x2 rigid supplied from Forbes of Aberdeen, was the start of a deluge as that Swedish marque became a Highland Haulage favourite. Into the 1970s, the F7 was to replace the F86 and Bill Mackenzie's retirement saw Norman Smith promoted to take over as Managing Director. The trunk service to Glasgow (soon supplemented by a service to Aberdeen) had grown to five or six vehicles every night and the upgrading of the A9 meant the hard-working drivers of Highland could go there and back in a single shift. Such a prospect would have been unthinkable 20 years earlier with, for example, an ageing Albion Reiver.

But this development in road technology was a bit of a double-edged sword. No longer did Inverness and beyond seem such a daunting prospect and increased competition meant Highland Haulage had to become more efficient. With the opening of Kessock Bridge over the Moray Firth, Conon Bridge was now hardly 20 minutes down the road from Inverness so the need for a depot there became unnecessary. The old smoke-house depot at Wick was also destined to close when costings of every sort came under scrutiny as the recession of the early 1980s came to Northern Scotland. A big drop in whisky consumption and the liquidation of a large timber customer were just two of the difficulties weathered by Highland Haulage. At least the examination showed that they had become a well-structured

Just as Highland Haulage were to Inverness and the North, so Connal and Co were long-established servants to the transport needs of Glasgow and the central belt of Scotland. This 1963 photograph of what was then their new vehicle park at the Maryhill depot illustrates the wide variety of types then in use and also some of the differing tasks. The two Albion artics in the left half of the picture were versions of the Chieftain Super Six which had the Leyland Comet six-cylinder engine rather than the standard Albion four-potter.

On October 1, 1986, the interests of Highland Haulage were merged with those of Connal and Co, and a new combined name was launched into the market-place. On their lighter range of multi-drop distribution vehicles, the company use both curtainsider and all-metal bodywork. Linkliner sliding metal doors are finding favour as being far quicker to open and close than the curtain-buckling procedure. This Scania 82 has curtains, though, and currently works out of Glasgow delivering oil and grease products widely in the central belt and border regions.

concern. Fleet size was to drop to about the 65 mark but this incorporated a far bigger payload potential in that number as well as an ability to reach far-flung destinations much more quickly.

But it was an overall costing strategy signalled by TDG that prompted the merger with Connal & Co and thus the disappearance of Highland Haulage as an entity. Connals had been particularly strong in the Glasgow dock area, having 110,000 square feet of warehousing at their 6-acre Maryhill site supplying loads for many vehicles which ran Highland bound. The coming together of these two parts of TDG was so appropriate that the merger on October 1, 1986 appeared just common sense.

Ex-Inverness man David Thomson now heads up the new Connal Highland Ltd. He is another example of the company's top man having worked his way through the ranks, starting off as a gopher at the age of 15. When he was promoted to Traffic Controller it was deemed to be a bonus to take his soon-to-be wife for a night run to Fort William in an old Albion loaded both ways with BOC gas bottles. He is now in charge of a fleet well into three figures run from a chain of six Scottish depots. With over 160 trailers, the company can offer flats, curtainsiders, fridge vans, skeletons, tail lifts, customer locked vans and even whisky tankers. The new combined concern is now fulfilling break bulk and order picking to complement their warehousing facilities. But no matter whether it's 900 tons of carbon blocks to Fort William, a crate to the Kyle of Lochalsh or a

he northern and western isles are still a
g part of the Connal Highland
stribution network, and the company
rrently has offices in both Lerwick and
rkwall. On dedicated contract to the
orth of Scotland Milk Marketing Board,
is Mercedes-Benz 1633S maximum-
eight reefer is used to haul cheese from
rkney to southern Scotland. Originally it
n as a fixed outfit but currently only the
mi-trailer is shipped on the ferry
etween Scrabster and Stromness.

ike many firms at the time, Connal
ighland first opted for the 2+3 axle
onfiguration when the 38 tonnes
gislation came into force, but they have
ow moved towards the 3+3 six-axled
utfit. Curtainsider bodywork is also well
ked, trailer number T26 being a Boalloy
onversion on what was originally a
lontracon platform. There is a weight
isadvantage with this type of outfit,
hough, and some Inverness-sourced traffic
till demands the lightest Volvo FL10 4x2
ractor unit coupled to a tri-axle flat to
nsure maximum payload.

couple of tons of car oil to the Orkneys, the framework
created by the old Highland Haulage means it's a service
that the company will regularly perform.

If anyone needed confirmation of Connal Highland's
continued commitment to the far-flung outposts of
Northern Scotland, it came in May 1990. It was then
announced that the Islands Division of Sutherlands
Transport Services and its 28 vehicles were transferred
from that TDG company across to Connal Highland, a

further twist in the interrelated histories of the region's
hauliers. And as a result of further restructuring and
rationalization amongst the component parts of the
Transport Development Group, more changes are in the
pipeline. At the time of writing, in early 1991, it seems that
the Connal Highland name will also disappear and the title
of another TDG concern, Inter City Transport, which had
its origins in Cumbernauld, will be the new banner for this
much-altered Inverness-based fleet.

15: Sunter Bros Ltd

Heavy haulage is an awe-inspiring aspect of road transport. Minor miracles seem a regular part of daily life as the men in this branch of the business exert their machines to perform the hardest of tasks. Tonnages measured by the thousands have become regular payloads for an industry which has made a big contribution to the development of North Sea oil production in a country that sorely needed that black gold.

But that same country went through a big shakedown in the recession of the early 1980s with a resultant decimation of our heavy industrial base. Concurrently, advances in technology have contributed to a cut-back in the production of the kind of large engineering masterpieces which were once the bread and butter of heavy haulage. These circumstances together would have been bad enough to live with, but the hauliers were also being asked to make bigger and bigger investments in equipment not only to handle the traffic that was still being moved but also to comply with changing legislation which sometimes seemed to be making the transformation from the steam age to the 1990s in a single leap.

The whole accumulation of circumstances was bound to bring casualties. Whilst some of the smaller independents could survive by tightening the girth, the larger names found themselves at the mercy of overriding financial directives. Safeguarding profit margins and the interests of shareholders often dictated closures and mergers, and it was the latter course which brought about the demise of one famous heavy-haulage name, that of Sunters.

Sunter Bros Ltd still exists as a company but, having already merged with Wynns Heavy Haulage to form United Heavy Transport, they underwent a further regrouping in 1986 to create Econofreight United Transport Ltd. With its head office in South Bank Road, Middlesbrough, and another depot at Chasetown in the Midlands, Econofreight, under the current leadership of Managing Director Tom Llewellyn, is the largest heavy haulier in the UK and it record of international achievements puts the company on par with anyone else throughout the world. Many of the old Sunter staff have made a big contribution to the high standing of Econofreight, and vehicle followers will still be able to spot some of the ex-Sunter vehicles, now painted blue and white. But naturally the dropping of the Sunter name was a hard blow to the enthusiasts: to them, a visit to the yard on Boroughbridge Road, Northallerton, was a joy indeed – although arguably it was railway travellers who got the best view of the depot as they sped by on the adjacent main-line track.

In fairness it could be said that Northallerton wasn't the best location for a heavy haulage concern of Sunters' magnitude although it was only very rarely that any of their huge loads came anywhere near to base. For, like all involved in this heavyweight game, the Sunters men were used to working anywhere in the UK, Europe or even further afield to carry on a trade which they made into an art form – quite a change from their earliest activities. To retrace those days the clock has to be turned back to 1923 and the microscope pointed at the idyllic village of Gunnerside.

Like many before them, Thomas and Joseph Sunter had Henry Ford to thank for providing their first load carrier. This was a Model T, not a goods carrier originally but a convertible car adapted to carry cattle and assorted agricultural produce between the higher reaches of Swaledale in North Yorkshire and the big town of Richmond. The Ford even got as far as Newcastle, carrying furniture, but it was hard work and tyres were a daily nightmare. It was a reflection that things were looking up when the brothers could afford to buy second-hand replacements instead of stuffing the punctured originals with grass. In 1927, a petrol-engined Chevrolet was taken into use, the brothers fitting an interchangeable body stem on its back. As an alternative to the usual calf-carrying crate, a large covered box body was used to haul light or bulky traffic.

Even in this Yorkshire Dale backwater, competition was still fairly keen. So in search of more lucrative work the brothers turned to the forests, where moving trees up to 70ft long was how they first learnt their heavy-haulage craft. They also had to learn about artics when moving this sort of load and their very first flexible six-wheeler, based on a Bedford tractive unit and a trailer axle from a redundant Dennis chassis, was built in Gunnerside to a simple but crude Sunter design. A steel plate for a fifth wheel, a long tree for the trailer chassis – which could be adjusted for length – and a wire cable attached to a cab winding handle for a trailer brake were all combined to make a very hairy outfit. It only earned its keep because of dedicated drivers, and at this early 1930s stage of the Sunter story there enters one of the company's finest ambassadors. John Robinson only lived a couple of miles down the road at Low Row and the entire 50 years of his working life were to be spent solely in the employ of Sunters. For most of that time, the accolade of being top-dog driver was his without doubt.

operated by a strong right boot – provided your nose could stand the smell of burning Ferodo. The few rigids apart, the main expansion at Sunters was in the timber-carrying artics with both Karrier and International vehicles taken into use. But that use was often almost total abuse: descending hills like Sutton Bank fully loaded with timber, the trailer axle would be deliberately locked up to control the momentum of the rig as it literally sledged downhill. No wonder these outfits were quickly run into the ground on timber work.

1937 saw the first brand-new vehicle bought, and in 'Little Bomber' – VN 9948 – Sunters opted for an ERF. This motor was first given to Lennie Sunter with the instructions to look after it and not to go too deep into the forest. Even this new flagship didn't have the luxury of an electric starter. What it did have was beautiful steering geometry but this wasn't really appreciated until Sunters chose a DG Foden as their second brand-new vehicle and realized what an 'armstrong' job it was in comparison.

By the late 1930s, Sunters' fortunes were beginning to change. Their long-length artics were fairly unique in the area so when Fred Robinson had some long steel traffic that he couldn't handle on his conventional Stockton-based fleet,

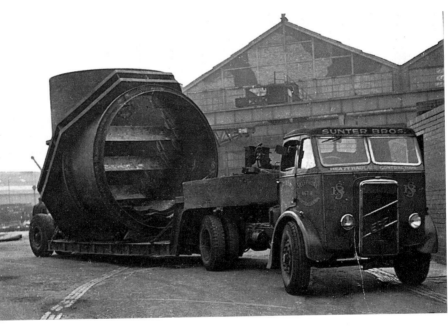

Affectionately known as 'Old Bomber', VN 9948 was the first brand-new ERF bought by the Sunter brothers and went into service in 1937. It was fitted with a Gardner 6LW engine, and its long wheelbase made it more akin to a tipper chassis than a tractor, a feature specified in order to increase stability when hauling long trees, its first staple traffic. It is seen in about 1946 about to leave Head Wrightsons at Thornaby coupled to a Hands low-loading semi-trailer.

Even at the illegal age of 16, John was driving the artic – until he got stopped for exceeding the 20mph speed limit near Aberford – along with another of the brothers, Lennie Sunter, who had also joined the family workforce. All combined to pull together, as an assortment of vehicles was brought into use. Some second-hand Albions came from Smiths Dock at South Bank but their drivers had to be very wary when they entered the forest. Catch a tree stump at the wrong angle with a front wheel and the steering system would snap just like that. A second-hand Leyland known as the Parkinson Pills van is also remembered for its idiosyncrasies. To compensate for a poor footbrake, the vehicle was fitted with a push-on handbrake which could be

he approached the Sunters to haul it on a subcontract basis. These loads were sourced out of Cargo Fleet on Teesside and a lot of it was destined for delivery into storage in London. This north/south delivery route was a long way east of Gunnerside and, with the timber wagons also working a long way from the Dales, the decision was made to move to a far more central location befitting the changing work pattern. Boroughbridge Road in Northallerton was chosen and the spot, ideally adjacent to the local railway station, was to be home for close on 50 years.

Although steel was a straightforward and lucrative cargo, timber was still very much the company's bread and butter. Any tree-moving work east of a line from about Barnard

Castle to Ripon, Sunters would be interested in. Their team needed a practised eye to identify the differing types of wood that were being cut. A lot went into John Spence, the Ripon timber merchant, but if it was beech then that was taken to the Snaith clog factory whilst larch was in big demand at the shipyards of Wallsend. During the wartime years the Sunter men turned up the pace, running the gauntlet of both bombers and the black-out. One regular task was taking awkwardly wide fabrications from the Malleable works at Stockton up to Dumbarton. Even running home empty, it was still a hard two-day job, but the carrot being dangled was the £3 a load being offered if three loads were moved in a week. This was a big jump in the pay packet when compared to the flat rate for 48 hours of £4 12s.

Work was to take on a heavier aspect after 1943 when the first low-loading semi-trailer, made by Hands, was brought into use. Lennie Sunter was credited with dreaming up this idea, although an inspiration by Tom to fit super sing tyres in place of twins wasn't as well accepted. Scamme Lorries were already doing this in their range but the b trouble started when you had to try and change a puncture wheel unassisted. Dropping the spare from the trail platform wasn't a problem, but lifting the punctured ma 4ft 6in off the ground was close to impossible. Overhangin branches were a driver's best friend, for by throwing a ro over and securing one end to the wagon, the other to th stricken wheel, forward motion lifted the tyre high enoug so that it could be swung inboard.

New vehicles arriving during the 1940s were CAJ 82 and 824, ERFs with five-pot Gardners in, plus CPY 744, Maudslay fitted with a 7.7-litre AEC engine. The latter wa given new to Phillip Braithwaite who had come to Sunte in 1938 as a 14-year-old timber tractor driver. Phillip recal that the Maudslay, which ran a lot of long steel, served hir well, with brakes well up to scratch. However, with it

After denationalization, when they had started up again, the Sunter brothers bought a batch of these AEC Mammoth Majors through Oswald Tillotson, the Burnley-based distributor for the marque. It was the dealer who chopped the six-wheelers down to tractor length: originally, they were all general haulage versions. The semi-trailer shown had also been worked on, the 45ft deck having started out as a Fruehauf step-frame. The somewhat weathered outfit is pictured in 1961 about to leave the Distington Engineering plant in Workington.

e Bradwell job was a major turning
int for Sunters, their loyal staff showing
at fantastic feats they were capable of.
238 tons each and 22ft in diameter, the
boilers that had to be moved would not
particularly unusual by 1990s standards,
t in 1957 the haul was entering uncharted
rritory. The first boiler established the
attern for what was to follow, and all eyes
ere on driver John Robinson as he set out
r the power station. Here, he is still
aded by one of the two factory Rotinoffs
hich were brought across to Essex to
emonstrate their mettle on this pull.

hilst the Rotinoff would naturally
vershadow all the other Sunters' tractors
r sheer drama, the 100-ton Foden took
me beating for dependability and
edication to its task. It would never win
ny races but drivers like Jack Emms swore
y its prowess. This Alan Simpson
hotograph shows the Foden, then almost
0 years old, leaving Thornaby on April 1,
964. Of equal note is the drawbar trailer,
s landing skids (not legs) indicating that it
as one of two 10ft-wide Dysons intended
riginally for export because they were 2ft
oo wide for normal UK operations.

exhaust manifold mounted on the nearside, rather than
close to the driver's leg on the offside, it was a particularly
cold wagon during the winter months.

Sunters' first six-wheeled artic tractor unit was DPY 447,
a double-drive ERF with Gardner 6LW engine that Jack
Thompson piloted. The vehicle was hardly run-in,
however, before it and the rest of the Sunter fleet were
swallowed up in the nationalization plan. This body-blow to
the brothers was only made bearable because they quickly
threw their energies into bus and taxi work, and for the next
three years the family traded under the name of Broadway

Coaches to keep their transport interests alive. A big source
of passenger traffic was actually right on the doorstep with
masses of conscripts flowing in and out of Catterick
Garrison on weekend leave. As people-carriers, Sunters
were to use a wide variety of makes including Guy, Foden,
AEC, Guildford and Crossley. Quickest across the ground
was a Beccles-bodied Leyland, its top speed of 75mph
contrasting with the snail-like progress of a narrow-bodied
Ford from which passengers had to dismount if the incline
got too steep. But whilst Broadway did quite well, even
prompting the creation of an extra depot at Catterick, the

Unlike Wynns, their sister company in t[...] Bulwark United organization, Sunte[...] never made extensive use of the Diamo[...] T, though they owned several. TUP 5 a[...] VPT 85 were bought from Crook [...] Willington Carriers in 1957. 998 BV[...] joined the fleet in 1962 and, in this scen[...] Jimmy Goulding is at the wheel some thr[...] years later, about to leave the Workingt[...] factory of Distington Engineering. Pet[...] Keenan is looking back as Georg[...] Wrightson examines the rear bogie. Th[...] was one of two Crane 30-ton-capacity uni[...] used on this job. Carrying the pontoo[...] which was 90ft long, 10ft high and 6ft wid[...] across to Birkenhead was made a litt[...] easier by the excellent hydraulic steerin[...] fitted to these bogies.

news of denationalization in road haulage was joy to the Sunters' ears.

Saying it was 'business as usual' may not have been quite true, as the brothers now emphasized their interest in heavy haulage, with Scammells being bought instead of the ERFs favoured earlier. KVN 604 was their first new Meadows-powered Mountaineer, coupled to a Crane 60-ton float, and driver John Robinson was expected to haul almost anything on a vehicle that only had a capacity of about 45 tons. Grossing twice that figure wasn't unusual yet if Robinson dared to ring in for a double-head, there would be all hell let loose.

Up in the Dales, the Sunter brothers had long been known for their fiery tempers. In fact, many people knew them as Tommy or Len Fire, especially if they had felt the cut of their tongue. But the Sunter tongues didn't fire so much when NAJ 920, a 6x6 Constructor, and then PPY

264, their big 100-ton Foden, began to establish th[...] brothers in the heavyweight league. As a company motto[...] the expression 'Go anywhere, carry anything' was adopte[...] – they felt it was something they could really live up to[...] The new tools of the trade were only as good as thei[...] operators, of course, and tractor drivers like Robinson an[...] Jock Fraser proved their worth as business prospered. I[...] 1957, the decision was made to go limited. Calling it Sunte[...] Brothers Ltd was a slight misnomer as, along with Tom[...] Joseph and Len, the company also involved their siste[...] Rosa. It was a successful time and the late 1950s was to b[...] the era when Sunters of Northallerton were to make thei[...] mark in heavy-haulage folklore.

The story of Bradwell Power Station and how Sunters[...] moved the 12 Head Wrightson boilers has been told a[...] length in *Moving Mountains*. Even now, more than 30[...] years on, it still ranks as one massive achievement. In[...]

'Powered by Rolls-Royce' is the proud badge on the front of this Guy Invincible which regular driver Phillip Braithwaite recalls performing a whole range of different tasks for the haulier. This giant 'tyre', 24 tons in weight and 24ft in diameter, made at Thornaby and destined for the Consett Iron Company, wasn't unduly heavy but was particularly awkward to support on the hydraulically-operated tilt frame. When pensioned off, the Guy went on to internal work at Dorman Long and then is believed to have gone down to the Humber Bridge site for arduous local shunting on that magnificent construction project.

essence it was breaking new ground, for each huge boiler tipped the scales at 238 tons and each had to be pulled off a starting incline of 1 in 10. It's difficult to put Bradwell into true perspective but it did ensure that Sunters became a name to be reckoned with. It was also an occasion that pitched Rotinoff into the heavy haulage tractor scene and for the many people who watched and wondered, it made driver John Robinson into something of a superman, too.

A further boost to the strength of the fleet came when the brothers snapped up the firm of Crook & Willington Carriers after the death of its founder, Joe Elliott. The long-term prospects for the new company seemed to be looking well when Tom Sunter suddenly died in hospital in 1963. Suffering from bad eyesight, he had undergone a routine

Sunters' fortunes prospered and their feats grew legendary.

The Sunter fleet flagships were mostly from Scammell. John Robinson was given the task of running-in their two Super Constructors, 447 DPY and KVN 860E, and then their famous Mark 1 240-ton Contractor which was first registered TPY 675H and then rebuilt as YVN 308T. The Rotinoff continued to give excellent service but only after its original manual gearbox was replaced with a far better semi-automatic version of the type which was used in the big Scammells. It was Head Engineer Mike Piechocki who takes the credit for this installation in 1962. Without any plans or diagrams to go with the assortment of bits, he had been given the job by Lennie Sunter to do 'in his spare time'. Mike vividly recalls spending 288 hours on the

These two fleet stalwarts were also powered by Rolls-Royce engines and, when new in the mid-1950s, they were examples of the strongest heavy-haulage tractors being built in the UK. The Scammell Constructor NAJ 920 was celebrated for having been tested by *Commercial Motor* prior to delivery in 1955. The Rotinoff behind it, and these 200-ton-capacity Crane bogies, were later presented to the Science Museum at Wroughton, near Swindon, where they are now preserved. This Dennis Wompra photograph shows the outfit about to leave Ashmores in Stockton on July 1, 1967.

operation but the last thing anyone had expected was that he would die from a heart attack just after surgery. Although his brother Joseph had died some time earlier, Tom Sunter had continued to hold the reins tightly. On his death, the complications in the estate meant that a sell-up was inevitable. In May 1964, Bulwark United Transport Ltd announced the take-over of Sunter Bros Ltd in a cash deal reckoned at £290,172. It was also recorded that 40 special-type vehicles were involved in the deal. But the biggest worry of the Sunter staff was that they would be simply swallowed up into the Wynns Group who had also been taken over by BUT only three months earlier. In fact it was to be more than 20 years before that was discussed and, for the bulk of that time, Peter Sunter, son of Len, filled the role of Managing Director. Far from declining,

transplant, the biggest bugbear being the fitting of a special throttle cut-out valve which prevented the vehicle from moving before the air pressure in the gearbox was at the required level. Like Archimedes, Mike found the solution when he was in the bath, and the resulting installation proved to be faultless.

To go with the diverse range of tractors, Sunters also used a wide variety of trailers. Their 200-ton-capacity Crane solid-tyred bogies must have carried the most weight in their long stay at Northallerton, but the heavy-tractor men will probably tell you about SB3, the 32-wheeler 90-ton-capacity girder trailer which seemed to have a mind of its own.

In 1967, Sunters did their first haul into mainland Europe and within four years, Continental work was to

Leylands were never to figure strongly in the Sunter line-up, though the brothers did buy three of them complete with their carriers' licences from J. S. Hall of Thorpe Thewles. Perhaps best remembered was the Super Hippo AVN 751B. The Beaver in this Dennis Wompra photograph from October 9, 1965 had been bought new three years earlier. Bobby Evans is at the wheel and the outfit is nearing its destination, hauling a 15ft-diameter vessel from Hull up to ICI Wilton.

become 10% of the company turnover. This was a basis on which Sunters were to develop this type of traffic and until well into the 1980s, the fleet were just as at ease in southern Germany, northern Sweden or the depths of Yorkshire. Working the Continent were vehicles of mainly Swedish manufacture as Volvos and Scania were taken into use for the light-middleweight range of traffic. Some odd exceptions included NPY 63F, a rare bonneted 6x4 tractor built by Atkinson to Peter Sunter's own specification. With a Cummins NH250 engine driving through an Allison six-speed automatic gearbox, it was built to work hard rather than look nice. It was intended originally as an artic tractor unit but a powerhouse ability meant it was soon converted into ballast-box guise.

The final Foden to come to Northallerton was WVN 181K, an S40-based 6x4 artic unit that was the pride and joy of dedicated Foden man Tony Swan. But the Foden didn't stay too long as the 1970s were the boom time for Sunters, their Scammells and, with a tie-up to ITM, modular movements at weights that were previously unthinkable. Later, Peter Sunter bucked convention when he imported their first German-built Titan which was to make the headlines until even that was dwarfed by the arrival of their famous Tractomas. Albert Lowes was its normal chauffeur and other big driving names of the time were Peter Clemmett, Bill Jemison, Jimmy Goulding, Ken

It is always something special to watch the heavy-haulage men having to double, treble or even, as in this case, quadruple-head their load to clear an incline. Early one Tuesday morning in July 1965, Henry Wood recorded this memorable sight on Cut Bank in Newcastle, all the fuss being created by a 200-ton ammonia convertor on solid-tyred bogies. The load was en route from West Germany to ICI Billingham and was one of three similar units which Sunters moved from the shipyard unloading point on the Tyne.

Sunters ran more than a score of different Atkinsons in their time but NPY 63F was the most individual of the breed. It was custom-built to Peter Sunter's specification and had an Allison automatic gearbox behind the Cummins engine. It is seen at Haywards Heath in 1972 taking one of six railway coaches to Sheffield Park for the Bluebell Line. Bob Caygill is driving the Atky whilst the balding Philip Braithwaite supervises the manoeuvre.

Into the late 1970s, the concept of modular trailers was to play a big part in heavy-haulage development. Trailer man John Easton, on the left, and driver Tony Swan are seen during November 1978 at the Nicolas factory in France where they went to collect 11 rows of new running gear. The Volvo, OVN 676R, was acquired specifically to haul empty running gear around the country, and sported a ballast box built by trailer fitter and blacksmith Peter Oldfield.

Bickerton and Malcolm Johnson. Modular load-carriers needed craftsmen on the trailers too, and these were to include Ivan Costik, John Garrett and, legend in his own lifetime, John Easton.

But no matter how good the men or the machines, the circumstances of the 1980s brought the curtain down on this fine North Yorkshire haulier. On May 16, 1986, United Heavy Transport Ltd (Sunter and Wynns) merged with Econofreight Transport Ltd. Even this situation was fairly unusual because at the outset the new company was jointly owned by BET and TDG, who, in essence, are two transport-owning conglomerates who are normally in direct competition with each other. The loss of the Sunter name, like many others from the transport scene, should be put into true perspective. In this ever-changing world nothing can be taken for granted. All that can be said is that they, like many others, have made a fine contribution to a service industry that this land of ours couldn't do without.

Fleet list

Sunter Bros Ltd

Vehicles in use around 1983-4

Fleet no	Reg no	Make/model	Axles	Type*
197	HVN 397N	Scammell Contractor	6x4	BT
198	LAJ 798P	Scammell Contractor	6x4	BT
303	NAJ 103P	Scammell Contractor	6x4	BT
306	OVN 676R	Volvo F89	6x4	A
307	VVN 910S	Titan	6x4	A
308	YVN 308T	Scammell Contractor	6x4	BT
309	YPY 209T	Scania 141	6x4	A
310	AVN 310T	Volvo F12	4x2	A
311	AVN 311T	Volvo F12	4x2	A
312	AVN 312T	Volvo F12	6x4	A
313	DVN 313V	Scania 141	6x4	A
314	CAJ 314T	Scania 141	4x2	A
315	CAJ 315T	Scania 141	4x2	A
316	DVN 316V	Scania 141	6x4	A
317	FPY 317V	Scania 111	4x2	A
318	RDC 318X	Nicolas Tractomas	6x6	BT
319	RDC 319X	Volvo F12	6x4	BT
320	EJW 299V	Titan	6x6	BT
321	SDC 121X	Scania 142	4x2	A
322	SDC 122X	Scania 142	4x2	A
323	A323 FHN	Scania 142	4x2	A
	BVN 129J	Albion/Coles	6x4	mobile crane
	UAJ 349S	Bedford TK	4x2	tackle wagon

Types: A artic tractor unit; BT ballast tractor unit.

A fitting swansong for Sunters was transporting this 304-tonne vessel, at 221ft the longest load ever to have been moved by road at the time. At about 10am on March 25, 1984, photographer Mike Brown caught Albert Lowes and his Tractomas going straight through what had been the Red Lion roundabout at Norton. It was like carnival day on Teesside as the crowds gathered to watch the procession make the six-mile journey from Thornaby to Billingham. Malcolm Johnson in Sunters' Titan 2 is the pusher at the rear: both he and Ken Bickerton in the other Titan hooked on to the front of the Tractomas for the hefty ascent of Billingham Bank.